American Constitution
Powers and Liberties

Sixth Edition

2 Supplement

2022 Supplement

American Constitutional Law: Powers and Liberties

Sixth Edition

Calvin R. Massey

Late Daniel Webster Distinguished Professor of Law
University of New Hampshire Law School
Professor of Law, Emeritus
University of California
Hastings College of Law

Brannon P. Denning

Starnes Professor of Law
Cumberland School of Law
Samford University

ASPEN PUBLISHING

ISBN 978-1-5438-0945-9

About Aspen Publishing

Aspen Publishing is a leading provider of educational content and digital learning solutions to law schools in the U.S. and around the world. Aspen provides best-in-class solutions for legal education through authoritative textbooks, written by renowned authors, and breakthrough products such as Connected eBooks, Connected Quizzing, and PracticePerfect.

The Aspen Casebook Series (famously known among law faculty and students as the "red and black" casebooks) encompasses hundreds of highly regarded textbooks in more than eighty disciplines, from large enrollment courses, such as Torts and Contracts to emerging electives such as Sustainability and the Law of Policing. Study aids such as the *Examples & Explanations* and the *Emanuel Law Outlines* series, both highly popular collections, help law students master complex subject matter.

Major products, programs, and initiatives include:

- **Connected eBooks** are enhanced digital textbooks and study aids that come with a suite of online content and learning tools designed to maximize student success. Designed in collaboration with hundreds of faculty and students, the Connected eBook is a significant leap forward in the legal education learning tools available to students.
- **Connected Quizzing** is an easy-to-use formative assessment tool that tests law students' understanding and provides timely feedback to improve learning outcomes. Delivered through CasebookConnect.com, the learning platform already used by students to access their Aspen casebooks, Connected Quizzing is simple to implement and integrates seamlessly with law school course curricula.
- **PracticePerfect** is a visually engaging, interactive study aid to explain commonly encountered legal doctrines through easy-to-understand animated videos, illustrative examples, and numerous practice questions. Developed by a team of experts, PracticePerfect is the ideal study companion for today's law students.
- The **Aspen Learning Library** enables law schools to provide their students with access to the most popular study aids on the market across all of their courses. Available through an annual subscription, the online library consists of study aids in e-book, audio, and video formats with full text search, note-taking, and highlighting capabilities.
- Aspen's **Digital Bookshelf** is an institutional-level online education bookshelf, consolidating everything students and professors need to ensure success. This program ensures that every student has access to affordable course materials from day one.
- **Leading Edge** is a community centered on thinking differently about legal education and putting those thoughts into actionable strategies. At the core of the program is the Leading Edge Conference, an annual gathering of legal education thought leaders looking to pool ideas and identify promising directions of exploration.

Contents

Table of Cases

American Constitutional Law: Powers and Liberties

Sixth Edition

2022 Supplement

Chapter 2

Doctrines Limiting the Scope of Judicial Review

C. Justiciability: The Proper Role of Federal Courts

2. Standing to Sue

a. The Constitutional Core of Standing

Page 84: Insert before the final paragraph in note 1.a.:

On the other hand, an attorney seeking to challenge provisions of the Maryland Constitution that required partisan balance in its courts on the ground that the provisions discriminated against him as a registered independent was found to lack standing because his claim was both a generalized grievance *and* he had not established he was "able and ready" to apply for vacant judicial positions. Carney v. Adams, 141 S. Ct. 493 (2020).

Page 84: Insert at the end of note 1.b.:

The Court elaborated on what constituted "concrete" harm in TransUnion, LLC v. Ramirez, 141 S. Ct. 2190 (2021). At issue was another class action alleging violation of the Fair Credit Reporting Act. The named plaintiff was denied the purchase of a car when, following a credit report furnished to the dealership by TransUnion, he was told his name was on a "watch list" maintained by the U.S. Treasury's Office of Foreign Assets Control. The notice was erroneous and was later removed by TransUnion. Rameriz sued and successfully certified a class action of more than 8,000 individuals who alleged that TransUnion had violated the FCRA by its failure to comply with "statutory obligations (i) to follow reasonable procedures to ensure the accuracy of credit files so that the files would not include OFAC alerts labeling the plaintiffs as potential terrorists; and (ii) to provide a consumer, upon request, with his or her complete credit file, including a summary of rights." The Court emphasized that merely because Congress has given individuals certain statutory rights, they still must demonstrate that the defendant's actions harmed them in a personal and tangible way. As to the first claim, the Court concluded that only those persons whose inaccurate credit reports were transmitted to third-parties had standing to pursue those claims. For the remaining class members whose inaccurate reports were not disseminated to anyone during the class period, the potential risk of future harm — which never materialized — was insufficient to support standing. As for the second claim, the Court held that Ramirez was the *only* member of the class who was able to prove he was harmed by the failure to comply with the copy-of-complete-file and summary-of-rights requirements. Four justices dissented in an unusual line up in which Justices Breyer, Sotomayor, and Kagan joined Justice Thomas's opinion.

Page 87: Insert at the end of the first paragraph in note 1.d.:

That said, the Court recently held that a plaintiff's injury can be satisfied — and the constitutional requirements for standing met — even if the plaintiff seeks only nominal damages. Uzuegbunam v. Presczewski, 141 S. Ct. 792 (2021).

4. Political Questions

Page 120: Insert a new paragraph at the end of note 1.b.:

The Court finally cut the Gordian Knot in Rucho v. Common Cause, 139 S. Ct. 2484 (2019), and held that partisan gerrymanders were nonjusticiable. The real issue in partisan gerrymanders, the Court held, was not whether a jurisdiction had engaged in partisan gerrymanders, but whether political gerrymandering had gone "too far"; it concluded that there were no judicially discoverable and manageable standards for making such a determination. Four Justices dissented.

Chapter 5

Separation of Powers

B. Executive Action

1. In Domestic Affairs

b. The Removal Power

Page 359: Insert a new note 3, renumber note 3 to note 4:

3. Seila Law LLC: Strengthening the Removal Power? In light of the 2008 financial crisis, Congress created the Consumer Finance Protection Bureau (CFPB), an agency tasked with policing the offering of consumer debt products and administering 19 consumer protection statutes. It was given broad rule-making, adjudicatory, enforcement, and investigatory powers. At its head was a single Director, appointed by the President with the advice and consent of the Senate — a principle officer, in other words. The Director, moreover, was removable by the President for inefficiency, neglect, or malfeasance only. When the Director ordered Seila Law, a law firm that offered debt relief services to its clients, to produce information and documents related to its practice, it sued seeking to have the demand set aside on the grounds that the for-cause removal provision violated separation of powers principles. Five members of the Court held that it did. Seila Law LLC v. Consumer Financial Protection Bureau, 140 S. Ct. 2183 (2020).

Writing that "the President's removal power is the rule, not the exception," Chief Justice Roberts observed that the removal power had been limited in only two instances. First, in *Humphrey's Executor*, which "permitted Congress to give for-cause removal protections to a multimember body of experts, balanced along partisan lines, that performed legislative and judicial functions and was said not to exercise any executive power." Second, in cases like *Morrison*, which recognized an exception for "inferior officers with limited duties and no policy-making or administrative authority . . . ." He continued:

> Neither *Humphrey's Executor* nor *Morrison* resolves whether the CFPB Director's insulation from removal is constitutional. Start with *Humphrey's*

Executor. Unlike the New Deal-era FTC upheld there, the CFPB is led by a single Director who cannot be described as a "body of experts" and cannot be considered "non-partisan" in the same sense as a group of officials drawn from both sides of the aisle. Moreover, while the staggered terms of the FTC Commissioners prevented complete turnovers in agency leadership and guaranteed that there would always be some Commissioners who had accrued significant expertise, the CFPB's single-Director structure and five-year term guarantee abrupt shifts in agency leadership and with it the loss of accumulated expertise.

In addition, the CFPB Director is hardly a mere legislative or judicial aid. Instead of making reports and recommendations to Congress, as the 1935 FTC did, the Director possesses the authority to promulgate binding rules fleshing out 19 federal statutes, including a broad prohibition on unfair and deceptive practices in a major segment of the U. S. economy. And instead of submitting recommended dispositions to an Article III court, the Director may unilaterally issue final decisions awarding legal and equitable relief in administrative adjudications. Finally, the Director's enforcement authority includes the power to seek daunting monetary penalties against private parties on behalf of the United States in federal court—a quintessentially executive power not considered in *Humphrey's Executor.*

The logic of *Morrison* also does not apply. Everyone agrees the CFPB Director is not an inferior officer, and her duties are far from limited. Unlike the independent counsel, who lacked policymaking or administrative authority, the Director has the sole responsibility to administer 19 separate consumer-protection statutes that cover everything from credit cards and car payments to mortgages and student loans. It is true that the independent counsel in *Morrison* was empowered to initiate criminal investigations and prosecutions, and in that respect wielded core executive power. But that power, while significant, was trained inward to high-ranking Governmental actors identified by others, and was confined to a specified matter in which the Department of Justice had a potential conflict of interest. By contrast, the CFPB Director has the authority to bring the coercive power of the state to bear on millions of private citizens and businesses, imposing even billion-dollar penalties through administrative adjudications and civil actions.

In light of these differences, the constitutionality of the CFPB Director's insulation from removal cannot be settled by *Humphrey's Executor* or *Morrison* alone.

Chief Justice Roberts noted that the Framers took care in the Constitution to "divide power everywhere except for the Presidency, and render the President directly accountable to the people through regular elections In that scheme, individual executive officials will wield significant authority, but that authority remains subject to the ongoing supervision and control of the elected President." Having a single Director of the CFPB subject only to for-cause removal "contravenes this carefully calibrated system by vesting significant governmental power in the hands of a single individual accountable to no one." He noted that the Director's five-year term meant that "some Presidents may not have any opportunity to shape [the CFPB's] leadership and thereby influence its activities" and that the Bureau was not even dependent on Congress for its operating budget, being funded by the Federal Reserve. A plurality then held that despite the constitutional infirmity of the for-cause provision, it could be severed and the Bureau continue in operation. Justices Thomas and Gorsuch dissented on the severability issue.

Justices Kagan, Ginsburg, Breyer, and Sotomayor agreed that the provision was severable, but dissented from the majority's invalidation of the for-cause provision. She wrote:

> Throughout the Nation's history, this Court has left most decisions about how to structure the Executive Branch to Congress and the President, acting through legislation they both agree to. In particular, the Court has commonly allowed those two branches to create zones of administrative independence by limiting the President's power to remove agency heads. The Federal Reserve Board. The Federal Trade Commission (FTC). The National Labor Relations Board. Statute after statute establishing such entities instructs the President that he may not discharge their directors except for cause — most often phrased as inefficiency, neglect of duty, or malfeasance in office. Those statutes, whose language the Court has repeatedly approved, provide the model for the removal restriction before us today. If precedent were any guide, that provision would have survived its encounter with this Court — and so would the intended independence of the Consumer Financial Protection Bureau (CFPB).
>
> Our Constitution and history demand that result. The text of the Constitution allows these common for-cause removal limits. Nothing in it speaks of removal. And it grants Congress authority to organize all the institutions of American governance, provided only that those arrangements allow the President to perform his own constitutionally assigned duties. Still more, the Framers' choice to give the political branches wide discretion over administrative offices has played out through American history in ways that have settled the constitutional meaning. From the first, Congress debated and enacted measures to create spheres of administration — especially of financial affairs — detached from direct presidential control. As the years passed, and governance became ever more complicated, Congress continued to adopt and adapt such measures — confident it had latitude to do so under a Constitution meant to "endure for ages to come." Not every innovation in governance — not every experiment in administrative independence — has proved successful. And debates about the prudence of limiting the President's control over regulatory agencies, including through his removal power, have never abated. But the Constitution — both as originally drafted and as practiced — mostly leaves disagreements about administrative structure to Congress and the President, who have the knowledge and experience needed to address them. Within broad bounds, it keeps the courts — who do not — out of the picture.

C.   Legislative Action and the Administrative State

2.   Specific Limits

a. Nondelegation

Page 412: Insert a new paragraph at the end of note 1:

The Court recently reaffirmed the intelligible principle test in a case challenging the authority of the Attorney General to determine whether sex offenders convicted prior to the passage of the Sex Offender Registration and Notification Act (SORNA) were required to comply with its registration requirements. Gundy v. United States, 139 S. Ct. 2116 (2019). A plurality of the Court determined that Congress's charge to the Attorney General to apply SORNA's registration requirement to all pre-enactment defendants as soon as was "feasible" met the standard. Justice Alito concurred, but indicated a willingness to reconsider the scope of the non-delegation doctrine in a future case. Justice Gorsuch dissented, joined by Chief Justice Roberts and Justice Thomas. In a lengthy opinion, Justice Gorsuch described the Court's adoption of the intelligible principles test as a "misadventure" and urged the Court to enforce the nondelegation doctrine in a more robust manner. Justice Kavanaugh did not participate in the case. It is possible that a future Court will return to this question in an appropriate case.

Chapter 6

Due Process

B. Substantive Due Process

3. The Modern Revival: "Privacy" Rights

b. Abortion

Omit pages 498-533; Insert after subsection b:

DOBBS v. JACKSON WOMEN'S
HEALTH ORGANIZATION
Supreme Court of the United States.
2022 WL 2276808

JUSTICE ALITO delivered the opinion of the Court.

Abortion presents a profound moral issue on which Americans hold sharply conflicting views. Some believe fervently that a human person comes into being at conception and that abortion ends an innocent life. Others feel just as strongly that any regulation of abortion invades a woman's right to control her own body and prevents women from achieving full equality. Still others in a third group think that abortion should be allowed under some but not all circumstances, and those within this group hold a variety of views about the particular restrictions that should be imposed.

For the first 185 years after the adoption of the Constitution, each State was permitted to address this issue in accordance with the views of its citizens. Then, in 1973, this Court decided. Even though the Constitution makes no mention of abortion, the Court held that it confers a broad right to obtain one. It did not claim that American law or the common law had ever recognized such a right, and its survey of history ranged from the constitutionally irrelevant (*e.g.*, its discussion of abortion in antiquity) to the plainly incorrect (*e.g.*, its assertion that abortion was probably never a crime under the common law). After cataloging a wealth

7

of other information having no bearing on the meaning of the Constitution, the opinion concluded with a numbered set of rules much like those that might be found in a statute enacted by a legislature.

Under this scheme, each trimester of pregnancy was regulated differently, but the most critical line was drawn at roughly the end of the second trimester, which, at the time, corresponded to the point at which a fetus was thought to achieve "viability," *i.e.*, the ability to survive outside the womb. Although the Court acknowledged that States had a legitimate interest in protecting "potential life," it found that this interest could not justify any restriction on pre-viability abortions. The Court did not explain the basis for this line, and even abortion supporters have found it hard to defend *Roe*'s reasoning. One prominent constitutional scholar wrote that he "would vote for a statute very much like the one the Court end[ed] up drafting" if he were "a legislator," but his assessment of *Roe* was memorable and brutal: *Roe* was "not constitutional law" at all and gave "almost no sense of an obligation to try to be."

At the time of *Roe*, 30 States still prohibited abortion at all stages. In the years prior to that decision, about a third of the States had liberalized their laws, but *Roe* abruptly ended that political process. It imposed the same highly restrictive regime on the entire Nation, and it effectively struck down the abortion laws of every single State. As Justice Byron White aptly put it in his dissent, the decision represented the "exercise of raw judicial power," and it sparked a national controversy that has embittered our political culture for a half century.

Eventually, in *Planned Parenthood of Southeastern Pa. v. Casey*, the Court revisited *Roe*, but the Members of the Court split three ways. Two Justices expressed no desire to change *Roe* in any way. Four others wanted to overrule the decision in its entirety. And the three remaining Justices, who jointly signed the controlling opinion, took a third position. Their opinion did not endorse *Roe*'s reasoning, and it even hinted that one or more of its authors might have "reservations" about whether the Constitution protects a right to abortion. But the opinion concluded that *stare decisis*, which calls for prior decisions to be followed in most instances, required adherence to what it called *Roe*'s "central holding" — that a State may not constitutionally protect fetal life before "viability" — even if that holding was wrong. Anything less, the opinion claimed, would undermine respect for this Court and the rule of law.

Paradoxically, the judgment in *Casey* did a fair amount of overruling. Several important abortion decisions were overruled *in toto*, and *Roe* itself was overruled in part. *Casey* threw out *Roe*'s trimester scheme and substituted a new rule of uncertain origin under which States were forbidden to adopt any regulation that imposed an "undue burden" on a woman's right to have an abortion. The decision provided no clear guidance about the difference between a "due" and an "undue" burden. But the three Justices who authored the controlling opinion "call[ed] the contending sides of a national controversy to end their national division" by treating the Court's decision as the final settlement of the question of the constitutional right to abortion.

As has become increasingly apparent in the intervening years, *Casey* did not achieve that goal. Americans continue to hold passionate and widely divergent views on abortion, and state legislatures have acted accordingly. Some have recently enacted laws allowing abortion, with few restrictions, at all stages of pregnancy. Others have tightly restricted abortion beginning well before viability. And in this case, 26 States have expressly asked this Court to overrule *Roe* and *Casey* and allow the States to regulate or prohibit pre-viability abortions.

Before us now is one such state law. The State of Mississippi asks us to uphold the constitutionality of a law that generally prohibits an abortion after the 15th week of pregnancy — several weeks before the point at which a fetus is now regarded as "viable" outside the womb. In defending this law, the State's primary argument is that we should reconsider and overrule *Roe* and *Casey* and once again allow each State to regulate abortion as its citizens wish. On the other side, respondents and the Solicitor General ask us to reaffirm *Roe* and *Casey*, and they contend that the Mississippi law cannot stand if we do so. Allowing Mississippi to prohibit abortions after 15 weeks of pregnancy, they argue, "would be no different than overruling *Casey* and *Roe* entirely." They contend that "no half-measures" are available and that we must either reaffirm or overrule *Roe* and *Casey*.

We hold that *Roe* and *Casey* must be overruled. The Constitution makes no reference to abortion, and no such right is implicitly protected by any constitutional provision, including the one on which the defenders of *Roe* and *Casey* now chiefly rely — the Due Process Clause of the Fourteenth Amendment. That provision has been held to guarantee some rights that are not mentioned in the Constitution, but any such right must be "deeply rooted in this Nation's history and tradition" and "implicit in the concept of ordered liberty."

The right to abortion does not fall within this category. Until the latter part of the 20th century, such a right was entirely unknown in American law. Indeed, when the Fourteenth Amendment was adopted, three quarters of the States made abortion a crime at all stages of pregnancy. The abortion right is also critically different from any other right that this Court has held to fall within the Fourteenth Amendment's protection of "liberty." *Roe*'s defenders characterize the abortion right as similar to the rights recognized in past decisions involving matters such as intimate sexual relations, contraception, and marriage, but abortion is fundamentally different, as both *Roe* and *Casey* acknowledged, because it destroys what those decisions called "fetal life" and what the law now before us describes as an "unborn human being."

Stare decisis, the doctrine on which *Casey*'s controlling opinion was based, does not compel unending adherence to *Roe*'s abuse of judicial authority. *Roe* was egregiously wrong from the start. Its reasoning was exceptionally weak, and the decision has had damaging consequences. And far from bringing about a national settlement of the abortion issue, *Roe* and *Casey* have enflamed debate and deepened division.

It is time to heed the Constitution and return the issue of abortion to the people's elected representatives. "The permissibility of abortion, and the limitations, upon it, are to be resolved like most important questions in our democracy: by citizens trying to persuade one another and then voting." That is what the Constitution and the rule of law demand. . . .

I. To support [the 15 week ban], the legislature made a series of factual findings. It began by noting that, at the time of enactment, only six countries besides the United States "permit[ted] nontherapeutic or elective abortion-on-demand after the twentieth week of gestation." The legislature then found that at 5 or 6 weeks' gestational age an "unborn human being's heart begins beating"; at 8 weeks the "unborn human being begins to move about in the womb"; at 9 weeks "all basic physiological functions are present"; at 10 weeks "vital organs begin to function," and "[h]air, fingernails, and toenails . . . begin to form"; at 11 weeks "an unborn human being's diaphragm is developing," and he or she may "move about freely in the womb"; and at 12 weeks the "unborn human being" has "taken on 'the human form' in all relevant respects." It found that most abortions after 15 weeks employ "dilation and evacuation procedures which involve the use of surgical instruments to crush and tear the unborn child," and it concluded that the "intentional commitment of such acts for nontherapeutic or elective reasons is a barbaric practice, dangerous for the maternal patient, and demeaning to the medical profession." . . .

II. We begin by considering the critical question whether the Constitution, properly understood, confers a right to obtain an abortion. Skipping over that question, the controlling opinion in *Casey* reaffirmed *Roe*'s "central holding" based solely on the doctrine of *stare decisis*, but as we will explain, proper application of *stare decisis* required an assessment of the strength of the grounds on which *Roe* was based. . . .

A.1. The Constitution makes no express reference to a right to obtain an abortion, and therefore those who claim that it protects such a right must show that the right is somehow implicit in the constitutional text.

Roe, however, was remarkably loose in its treatment of the constitutional text. It held that the abortion right, which is not mentioned in the Constitution, is part of a right to privacy, which is also not mentioned. And that privacy right, *Roe* observed, had been found to spring from no fewer than five different constitutional provisions — the First, Fourth, Fifth, Ninth, and Fourteenth Amendments.

The Court's discussion left open at least three ways in which some combination of these provisions could protect the abortion right. One possibility was that the right was "founded . . . in the Ninth Amendment's reservation of rights to the people." Another was that the right was rooted in the First, Fourth, or Fifth Amendment, or in some combination of those provisions, and that this right had been "incorporated" into the Due Process Clause of the Fourteenth Amendment just as many other Bill of Rights provisions had by then been incorporated. And a third path was that the First, Fourth, and Fifth Amendments played no role and that the right was simply a component of the "liberty" protected by the

Fourteenth Amendment's Due Process Clause. *Roe* expressed the "feel[ing]" that the Fourteenth Amendment was the provision that did the work, but its message seemed to be that the abortion right could be found *somewhere* in the Constitution and that specifying its exact location was not of paramount importance. The *Casey* Court did not defend this unfocused analysis and instead grounded its decision solely on the theory that the right to obtain an abortion is part of the "liberty" protected by the Fourteenth Amendment's Due Process Clause. . . .

2. The underlying theory on which this argument rests—that the Fourteenth Amendment's Due Process Clause provides substantive, as well as procedural, protection for "liberty"—has long been controversial. But our decisions have held that the Due Process Clause protects two categories of substantive rights.

The first consists of rights guaranteed by the first eight Amendments. Those Amendments originally applied only to the Federal Government, but this Court has held that the Due Process Clause of the Fourteenth Amendment "incorporates" the great majority of those rights and thus makes them equally applicable to the States. The second category—which is the one in question here—comprises a select list of fundamental rights that are not mentioned anywhere in the Constitution.

In deciding whether a right falls into either of these categories, the Court has long asked whether the right is "deeply rooted in [our] history and tradition" and whether it is essential to our Nation's "scheme of ordered liberty." And in conducting this inquiry, we have engaged in a careful analysis of the history of the right at issue. . . .

Historical inquiries of this nature are essential whenever we are asked to recognize a new component of the "liberty" protected by the Due Process Clause because the term "liberty" alone provides little guidance. "Liberty" is a capacious term. As Lincoln once said: "We all declare for Liberty; but in using the same word we do not all mean the same thing." In a well-known essay, Isaiah Berlin reported that "[h]istorians of ideas" had cataloged more than 200 different senses in which the term had been used.

In interpreting what is meant by the Fourteenth Amendment's reference to "liberty," we must guard against the natural human tendency to confuse what that Amendment protects with our own ardent views about the liberty that Americans should enjoy. That is why the Court has long been "reluctant" to recognize rights that are not mentioned in the Constitution. . . .

B.1. Until the latter part of the 20th century, there was no support in American law for a constitutional right to obtain an abortion. No state constitutional provision had recognized such a right. Until a few years before *Roe* was handed down, no federal or state court had recognized such a right. Nor had any scholarly treatise of which we are aware. And although law review articles are not reticent about advocating new rights, the earliest article proposing a constitutional right to abortion that has come to our attention was published only a few years before *Roe*.

Not only was there no support for such a constitutional right until shortly before *Roe*, but abortion had long been a *crime* in every single State. At common law, abortion was criminal in at least some stages of pregnancy and was regarded as unlawful and could have very serious consequences at all stages. American law followed the common law until a wave of statutory restrictions in the 1800s expanded criminal liability for abortions. By the time of the adoption of the Fourteenth Amendment, three-quarters of the States had made abortion a crime at any stage of pregnancy, and the remaining States would soon follow. . . .

2.a. We begin with the common law, under which abortion was a crime at least after "quickening" — *i.e.*, the first felt movement of the fetus in the womb, which usually occurs between the 16th and 18th week of pregnancy. [Alito reviewed several English common law authorities, concluding:]

In sum, although common-law authorities differed on the severity of punishment for abortions committed at different points in pregnancy, none endorsed the practice. Moreover, we are aware of no common-law case or authority, and the parties have not pointed to any, that remotely suggests a positive *right* to procure an abortion at any stage of pregnancy.

b. In this country, the historical record is similar. The "most important early American edition of Blackstone's Commentaries," reported Blackstone's statement that abortion of a quick child was at least "a heinous misdemeanor," [and] [m]anuals for justices of the peace printed in the Colonies in the 18th century typically restated the common-law rule on abortion . . .

The few cases available from the early colonial period corroborate that abortion was a crime. . . .

c. [In the 19th century, Alito noted, the pre- and post-quickening rules were abandoned and states began to criminalize abortion at all stages of pregnancy.]

By 1868, the year when the Fourteenth Amendment was ratified, three-quarters of the States, 28 out of 37, had enacted statutes making abortion a crime even if it was performed before quickening. Of the nine States that had not yet criminalized abortion at all stages, all but one did so by 1910.

The trend in the Territories that would become the last 13 States was similar: All of them criminalized abortion at all stages of pregnancy between 1850 (the Kingdom of Hawaii) and 1919 (New Mexico). By the end of the 1950s, according to the *Roe* Court's own count, statutes in all but four States and the District of Columbia prohibited abortion "however and whenever performed, unless done to save or preserve the life of the mother."

This overwhelming consensus endured until the day *Roe* was decided. At that time . . . a substantial majority — 30 States — still prohibited abortion at all stages except to save the life of the mother. And though *Roe* discerned a "trend toward liberalization" in about "one-third of the States," those States still criminalized some abortions and regulated them more stringently than *Roe* would allow. . . .

d. The inescapable conclusion is that a right to abortion is not deeply rooted in the Nation's history and traditions. On the contrary, an unbroken tradition of prohibiting abortion on pain of criminal punishment persisted from the earliest days of the common law until 1973. . . .

3. Not only are respondents and their *amici* unable to show that a constitutional right to abortion was established when the Fourteenth Amendment was adopted, but they have found no support for the existence of an abortion right that predates the latter part of the 20th century — no state constitutional provision, no statute, no judicial decision, no learned treatise. The earliest sources called to our attention are a few district court and state court decisions decided shortly before *Roe* and a small number of law review articles from the same time period. . . .

C.1. Instead of seriously pressing the argument that the abortion right itself has deep roots, supporters of *Roe* and *Casey* contend that the abortion right is an integral part of a broader entrenched right. *Roe* termed this a right to privacy, and *Casey* described it as the freedom to make "intimate and personal choices" that are "central to personal dignity and autonomy," *Casey* elaborated: "At the heart of liberty is the right to define one's own concept of existence, of meaning, of the universe, and of the mystery of human life."

The Court did not claim that this broadly framed right is absolute, and no such claim would be plausible. W hile individuals are certainly free *to think* and *to say* what they wish about "existence," "meaning," the "universe," and "the mystery of human life," they are not always free *to act* in accordance with those thoughts. License to act on the basis of such beliefs may correspond to one of the many understandings of "liberty," but it is certainly not "ordered liberty." . . .

Roe and *Casey* each struck a particular balance between the interests of a woman who wants an abortion and the interests of what they termed "potential life." But the people of the various States may evaluate those interests differently. . . .

Nor does the right to obtain an abortion have a sound basis in precedent. [Alito noted that *Roe* cited cases involving everything from the right to obtain contraceptives to the right to live with relatives.]

These attempts to justify abortion through appeals to a broader right to autonomy and to define one's "concept of existence" prove too much. Those criteria, at a high level of generality, could license fundamental rights to illicit drug use, prostitution, and the like. None of these rights has any claim to being deeply rooted in history.

What sharply distinguishes the abortion right from the rights recognized in the cases on which *Roe* and *Casey* rely is something that both those decisions acknowledged: Abortion destroys what those decisions call "potential life" and what the law at issue in this case regards as the life of an "unborn human being." . . .

D.1. The dissent is very candid that it cannot show that a constitutional right to abortion has any foundation, let alone a " 'deeply rooted' " one, " 'in this Nation's history and tradition.' " . . .

The dissent's failure to engage with this long tradition is devastating to its position. We have held that the "established method of substantive-due-process analysis" requires that an unenumerated right be " 'deeply rooted in this Nation's history and tradition' " before it can be recognized as a component of the "liberty" protected in the Due Process Clause. . . .

2. Because the dissent cannot argue that the abortion right is rooted in this Nation's history and tradition, it contends that the "constitutional tradition" is "not captured whole at a single moment," and that its "meaning gains content from the long sweep of our history and from successive judicial precedents." This vague formulation imposes no clear restraints on what Justice White called the "exercise of raw judicial power," and while the dissent claims that its standard "does not mean anything goes," any real restraints are hard to discern. . . .

So without support in history or relevant precedent, *Roe*'s reasoning cannot be defended even under the dissent's proposed test, and the dissent is forced to rely solely on the fact that a constitutional right to abortion was recognized in *Roe* and later decisions that accepted *Roe*'s interpretation. . . .

3. The most striking feature of the dissent is the absence of any serious discussion of the legitimacy of the States' interest in protecting fetal life. . . . The exercise of the rights at issue in *Griswold*, *Eisenstadt*, *Lawrence*, and *Obergefell* does not destroy a "potential life," but an abortion has that effect. So if the rights at issue in those cases are fundamentally the same as the right recognized in *Roe* and *Casey*, the implication is clear: The Constitution does not permit the States to regard the destruction of a "potential life" as a matter of any significance. . . .

III. We next consider whether the doctrine of *stare decisis* counsels continued acceptance of *Roe* and *Casey*. . . .

We have long recognized . . . that *stare decisis* is "not an inexorable command," . . Therefore, in appropriate circumstances we must be willing to reconsider and, if necessary, overrule constitutional decisions. . . .

In this case, five factors weigh strongly in favor of overruling *Roe* and *Casey*: the nature of their error, the quality of their reasoning, the "workability" of the rules they imposed on the country, their disruptive effect on other areas of the law, and the absence of concrete reliance.

A. *The nature of the Court's error.* An erroneous interpretation of the Constitution is always important, but some are more damaging than others. . . .

Roe was on a collision course with the Constitution from the day it was decided, *Casey* perpetuated its errors, and those errors do not concern some arcane corner of the law of little importance to the American people. Rather, wielding nothing but "raw judicial power," the Court usurped the power to address a question of profound moral and social importance that the Constitution unequivocally leaves for the people. *Casey* described itself as calling both sides of the national controversy to resolve their debate, but in doing so, *Casey* necessarily declared a winning side. . . .

B. *The quality of the reasoning.* Under our precedents, the quality of the reasoning in a prior case has an important bearing on whether it should be reconsidered. . . .

Roe found that the Constitution implicitly conferred a right to obtain an abortion, but it failed to ground its decision in text, history, or precedent. It relied on an erroneous historical narrative; it devoted great attention to and presumably relied on matters that have no bearing on the meaning of the Constitution; it disregarded the fundamental difference between the precedents on which it relied and the question before the Court; it concocted an elaborate set of rules, with different restrictions for each trimester of pregnancy, but it did not explain how this veritable code could be teased out of anything in the Constitution, the history of abortion laws, prior precedent, or any other cited source; and its most important rule (that States cannot protect fetal life prior to "viability") was never raised by any party and has never been plausibly explained. *Roe*'s reasoning quickly drew scathing scholarly criticism, even from supporters of broad access to abortion.

The *Casey* plurality, while reaffirming *Roe*'s central holding, . . . replaced [the trimester framework] with an arbitrary "undue burden" test and relied on an exceptional version of *stare decisis* that, as explained below, this Court had never before applied and has never invoked since. . . .

C. *Workability*. Our precedents counsel that another important consideration in deciding whether a precedent should be overruled is whether the rule it imposes is workable—that is, whether it can be understood and applied in a consistent and predictable manner. *Casey*'s "undue burden" test has scored poorly on the workability scale. . . .

1. The *Casey* plurality tried to put meaning into the "undue burden" test by setting out three subsidiary rules, but these rules created their own problems. The first rule is that "a provision of law is invalid, if its purpose or effect is to place a *substantial obstacle* in the path of a woman seeking an abortion before the fetus attains viability." But whether a particular obstacle qualifies as "substantial" is often open to reasonable debate. In the sense relevant here, "substantial" means "of ample or considerable amount, quantity, or size." Huge burdens are plainly "substantial," and trivial ones are not, but in between these extremes, there is a wide gray area.

This ambiguity is a problem, and the second rule, which applies at all stages of a pregnancy, muddies things further. It states that measures designed "to ensure that the woman's choice is informed" are constitutional so long as they do not impose "an undue burden on the right." To the extent that this rule applies to pre-viability abortions, it overlaps with the first rule and appears to impose a different standard. Consider a law that imposes an insubstantial obstacle but serves little purpose. As applied to a pre-viability abortion, would such a regulation be constitutional on the ground that it does not impose a "*substantial* obstacle"? Or would it be unconstitutional on the ground that it creates an "*undue* burden" because the burden it imposes, though slight, outweighs its negligible benefits? *Casey* does not say, and this ambiguity would lead to confusion down the line.

The third rule complicates the picture even more. Under that rule, "*[u]nnecessary health* regulations that have the purpose or effect of presenting a *substantial obstacle* to a woman seeking an abortion impose an *undue burden* on the right." This rule contains no fewer than three vague terms. It includes the two already discussed—"undue burden" and "substantial obstacle"—even though they are inconsistent. And it adds a third ambiguous term when it refers to "*unnecessary* health regulations." . . . .

In addition to these problems, one more applies to all three rules. They all call on courts to examine a law's effect on women, but a regulation may have a very different impact on different women for a variety of reasons, including their places of residence, financial resources, family situations, work and personal obligations, knowledge about fetal development and abortion, psychological and emotional disposition and condition, and the firmness of their desire to obtain abortions. . . .

[Justice Alito noted that the Court has divided on whether the undue burden test implicitly incorporated an interest-balancing test that required courts to take account of burdens on access against the purported benefits of the law. The confusion engendered by the inability to settle that question, in turn, produced "a long list of Circuit conflicts."]

D. *Effect on other areas of law. Roe* and *Casey* have led to the distortion of many important but unrelated legal doctrines, and that effect provides further support for overruling those decisions. . . .

The Court's abortion cases have diluted the strict standard for facial constitutional challenges. They have ignored the Court's third-party standing doctrine. They have disregarded standard *res judicata* principles. They have flouted the ordinary rules on the severability of unconstitutional provisions, as well as the rule that statutes should be read where possible to avoid unconstitutionality. And they have distorted First Amendment doctrines.

E, *Reliance interests.* We last consider whether overruling *Roe* and *Casey* will upend substantial reliance interests.

1. Traditional reliance interests arise "where advance planning of great precision is most obviously a necessity." In *Casey*, the controlling opinion conceded that those traditional reliance interests were not implicated because getting an abortion is generally "unplanned activity," and "reproductive planning could take virtually immediate account of any sudden restoration of state authority to ban abortions." . . .

2. Unable to find reliance in the conventional sense, the controlling opinion in *Casey* perceived a more intangible form of reliance. It wrote that "people [had] organized intimate relationships and made choices that define their views of themselves and their places in society . . . in reliance on the availability of abortion in the event that contraception should fail" and that "[t]he ability of women to participate equally in the economic and social life of the Nation has been facilitated by their ability to control their reproductive lives." But this Court is ill-equipped to assess "generalized assertions about the national psyche." . . .

Our decision returns the issue of abortion to those legislative bodies, and it allows women on both sides of the abortion issue to seek to affect the legislative pro cess by influencing public opinion, lobbying legislators, voting, and running for office. . . . It is noteworthy that the percentage of women who register to vote and cast ballots is consistently higher than the percentage of men who do so. . . .

3. Unable to show concrete reliance on *Roe* and *Casey* themselves, the Solicitor General suggests that overruling those decisions would "threaten the Court's precedents holding that the Due Process Clause protects other rights." . . . As even the *Casey* plurality recognized, "[a]bortion is a unique act" because it terminates "life or potential life." And to ensure that our decision is not misunderstood or mischaracterized, we emphasize that our decision concerns the constitutional right to abortion and no other right. Nothing in this opinion should be understood to cast doubt on precedents that do not concern abortion.

IV. Having shown that traditional *stare decisis* factors do not weigh in favor of retaining *Roe* or *Casey*, we must address one final argument that featured prominently in the *Casey* plurality opinion.

The argument was cast in different terms, but stated simply, it was essentially as follows. The American people's belief in the rule of law would be shaken if they lost respect for this Court as an institution that decides important cases based on principle, not "social and political pressures." . . .

This analysis starts out on the right foot but ultimately veers off course. The *Casey* plurality was certainly right that it is important for the public to perceive that our decisions are based on principle, and we should make every effort to achieve that objective by issuing opinions that carefully show how a proper understanding of the law leads to the results we reach. But we cannot exceed the scope of our authority under the Constitution, and we cannot allow our decisions to be affected by any extraneous influences such as concern about the public's reaction to our work. . . .

The *Casey* plurality "call[ed] the contending sides of a national controversy to end their national division," and claimed the authority to impose a permanent settlement of the issue of a constitutional abortion right simply by saying that the matter was closed. That unprecedented claim exceeded the power vested in us by the Constitution. . . .

Neither [*Roe* nor *Casey*] has ended debate over the issue of a constitutional right to obtain an abortion. Indeed, in this case, 26 States expressly ask us to overrule *Roe* and *Casey* and to return the issue of abortion to the people and their elected representatives. . . .

V.A.1. The dissent argues that we have "abandon[ed]" *stare decisis*, but we have done no such thing, and it is the dissent's understanding of *stare decisis* that breaks with tradition. The dissent's foundational contention is that the Court should never (or perhaps almost never) overrule an egregiously wrong constitutional precedent unless the Court can "poin[t] to major legal or factual changes undermining [the] decision's original basis." To support this contention, the dissent claims that *Brown v. Board of Education*, and other landmark cases overruling prior precedents "responded to changed law and to changed facts and attitudes that had taken hold throughout society." The unmistakable implication of this argument is that only the passage of time and new developments justified those decisions. Recognition that the cases they overruled were egregiously wrong on the day they were handed down was not enough.

The Court has never adopted this strange new version of *stare decisis* — and with good reason. Does the dissent really maintain that overruling *Plessy* was not justified until the country had experienced more than a half-century of state-sanctioned segregation and generations of Black school children had suffered all its effects? . . .

VI. We must now decide what standard will govern if state abortion regulations undergo constitutional challenge and whether the law before us satisfies the appropriate standard.

A. Under our precedents, rational-basis review is the appropriate standard for such challenges. As we have explained, procuring an abortion is not a fundamental constitutional right because such a right has no basis in the Constitution's text or in our Nation's history. . . .

A law regulating abortion, like other health and welfare laws, is entitled to a "strong presumption of validity." It must be sustained if there is a rational basis on which the legislature could have thought that it would serve legitimate state interests. These legitimate interests include respect for and preservation of prenatal life at all stages of development; the protection of maternal health and safety; the elimination of particularly gruesome or barbaric medical procedures; the preservation of the integrity of the medical profession; the mitigation of fetal pain; and the prevention of discrimination on the basis of race, sex, or disability.

B. These legitimate interests justify Mississippi's Gestational Age Act. Except "in a medical emergency or in the case of a severe fetal abnormality," the statute prohibits abortion "if the probable gestational age of the unborn human being has been determined to be greater than fifteen (15) weeks." The Mississippi Legislature's findings recount the stages of "human prenatal development" and assert the State's interest in "protecting the life of the unborn." The legislature also found that abortions performed after 15 weeks typically use the dilation and evacuation procedure, and the legislature found the use of this procedure "for nontherapeutic or elective reasons [to be] a barbaric practice, dangerous for the maternal patient, and demeaning to the medical profession." These legitimate interests provide a rational basis for the Gestational Age Act, and it follows that respondents' constitutional challenge must fail.

VII. We end this opinion where we began. Abortion presents a profound moral question. The Constitution does not prohibit the citizens of each State from regulating or prohibiting abortion. *Roe* and *Casey* arrogated that authority. We now overrule those decisions and return that authority to the people and their elected representatives. . . .

It is so ordered.

JUSTICE THOMAS, concurring. . . .

Because the Court properly applies our substantive due process precedents to reject the fabrication of a constitutional right to abortion, and because this case does not present the opportunity to reject substantive due process entirely,

I join the Court's opinion. But, in future cases, we should "follow the text of the Constitution, which sets forth certain substantive rights that cannot be taken away, and adds, beyond that, a right to due process when life, liberty, or property is to be taken away." Substantive due process conflicts with that textual command and has harmed our country in many ways. Accordingly, we should eliminate it from our jurisprudence at the earliest opportunity.

JUSTICE KAVANAUGH, concurring.

III. After today's decision, the nine Members of this Court will no longer decide the basic legality of pre-viability abortion for all 330 million Americans. That issue will be resolved by the people and their representatives in the democratic process in the States or Congress. But the parties' arguments have raised other related questions, and I address some of them here.

First is the question of how this decision will affect other precedents involving issues such as contraception and marriage—in particular, the decisions in *Griswold v. Connecticut*; *Eisenstadt v. Baird*; *Loving v. Virginia*; and *Obergefell v. Hodges*. I emphasize what the Court today states: Overruling *Roe* does *not* mean the overruling of those precedents, and does *not* threaten or cast doubt on those precedents.

Second, as I see it, some of the other abortion-related legal questions raised by today's decision are not especially difficult as a constitutional matter. For example, may a State bar a resident of that State from traveling to another State to obtain an abortion? In my view, the answer is no based on the constitutional right to interstate travel. May a State retroactively impose liability or punishment for an abortion that occurred before today's decision takes effect? In my view, the answer is no based on the Due Process Clause or the *Ex Post Facto* Clause. . . .

CHIEF JUSTICE ROBERTS, concurring in the judgment. . . .

Today, the Court . . . rules for Mississippi by [overruling *Roe* and *Casey*]. I would take a more measured course. I agree with the Court that the viability line established by *Roe* and *Casey* should be discarded under a straightforward *stare decisis* analysis. That line never made any sense. Our abortion precedents describe the right at issue as a woman's right to choose to terminate her pregnancy. That right should therefore extend far enough to ensure a reasonable opportunity to choose, but need not extend any further—certainly not all the way to viability. Mississippi's law allows a woman three months to obtain an abortion, well beyond the point at which it is considered "late" to discover a pregnancy. . . .

But that is all I would say, out of adherence to a simple yet fundamental principle of judicial restraint: If it is not necessary to decide more to dispose of a case, then it is necessary *not* to decide more. Perhaps we are not always perfect in following that command, and certainly there are cases that warrant an exception. But this is not one of them. Surely we should adhere closely to principles of judicial restraint here, where the broader path the Court chooses entails repudiating a constitutional right we have not only previously recognized, but also expressly reaffirmed applying the doctrine of *stare decisis*. The Court's opinion is thoughtful and thorough, but those virtues cannot compensate for the fact that its dramatic and consequential ruling is unnecessary to decide the case before us. . . .

JUSTICE BREYER, JUSTICE SOTOMAYOR, and JUSTICE KAGAN, dissenting.

For half a century, *Roe v. Wade* and *Planned Parenthood of Southeastern Pa. v. Casey*, have protected the liberty and equality of women. *Roe* held, and *Casey* reaffirmed, that the Constitution safeguards a woman's right to decide for herself whether to bear a child. *Roe* held, and *Casey* reaffirmed, that in the first stages of pregnancy, the government could not make that choice for women. The government could not control a woman's body or the course of a woman's life: It could not determine what the woman's future would be. Respecting a woman as an autonomous being, and granting her full equality, meant giving her substantial choice over this most personal and most consequential of all life decisions.

Roe and *Casey* well understood the difficulty and divisiveness of the abortion issue. The Court knew that Americans hold profoundly different views about the "moral[ity]" of "terminating a pregnancy, even in its earliest stage." And the Court recognized that "the State has legitimate interests from the outset of the pregnancy in protecting" the "life of the fetus that may become a child." So the Court struck a balance, as it often does when values and goals compete. It held that the State could prohibit abortions after fetal viability, so long as the ban contained exceptions to safeguard a woman's life or health. It held that even before viability, the State could regulate the abortion procedure in multiple and meaningful ways. But until the viability line was crossed, the Court held, a State could not impose a "substantial obstacle" on a woman's "right to elect the procedure" as she (not the government) thought proper, in light of all the circumstances and complexities of her own life.

Today, the Court discards that balance. It says that from the very moment of fertilization, a woman has no rights to speak of. A State can force her to bring a pregnancy to term, even at the steepest personal and familial costs. An abortion restriction, the majority holds, is permissible whenever rational, the lowest level of scrutiny known to the law. And because, as the Court has often stated, protecting fetal life is rational, States will feel free to enact all manner of restrictions. The Mississippi law at issue here bars abortions after the 15th week of pregnancy. Under the majority's ruling, though, another State's law could do so after ten weeks, or five or three or one — or, again, from the moment of fertilization. States have already passed such laws, in anticipation of today's ruling. More will follow. Some States have enacted laws extending to all forms of abortion procedure, including taking medication in one's own home. They have passed laws without any exceptions for when the woman is the victim of rape or incest. Under those laws, a woman will have to bear her rapist's child or a young girl her father's — no matter if doing so will destroy her life. So too, after today's ruling, some States may compel women to carry to term a fetus with severe physical anomalies — for example, one afflicted with Tay-Sachs disease, sure to die within a few years of birth. States may even argue that a prohibition on abortion need make no provision for protecting a woman from risk of death or physical harm. Across a vast array of circumstances, a State will be able to impose its moral choice on a woman and coerce her to give birth to a child.

Enforcement of all these draconian restrictions will also be left largely to the States' devices. A State can of course impose criminal penalties on abortion providers, including lengthy prison sentences. But some States will not stop there. Perhaps, in the wake of today's decision, a state law will criminalize the woman's conduct too, incarcerating or fining her for daring to seek or obtain an abortion. And as Texas has recently shown, a State can turn neighbor against neighbor, enlisting fellow citizens in the effort to root out anyone who tries to get an abortion, or to assist another in doing so.

The majority tries to hide the geographically expansive effects of its holding. Today's decision, the majority says, permits "each State" to address abortion as it pleases. That is cold comfort, of course, for the poor woman who cannot get the money to fly to a distant State for a procedure. Above all others, women lacking financial resources will suffer from today's decision. In any event, interstate restrictions will also soon be in the offing. After this decision, some States may block women from traveling out of State to obtain abortions, or even from receiving abortion medications from out of State. Some may criminalize efforts, including the provision of information or funding, to help women gain access to other States' abortion services. Most threatening of all, no language in today's decision stops the Federal Government from prohibiting abortions nationwide, once again from the moment of conception and without exceptions for rape or incest. If that happens, "the views of [an individual State's] citizens" will not matter. The challenge for a woman will be to finance a trip not to "New York [or] California" but to Toronto.

Whatever the exact scope of the coming laws, one result of today's decision is certain: the curtailment of women's rights, and of their status as free and equal citizens. Yesterday, the Constitution guaranteed that a woman confronted with an unplanned pregnancy could (within reasonable limits) make her own decision about whether to bear a child, with all the life-transforming consequences that act involves. And in thus safeguarding each woman's reproductive freedom, the Constitution also protected "[t]he ability of women to participate equally in [this Nation's] economic and social life." But no longer. As of today, this Court holds, a State can always force a woman to give birth, prohibiting even the earliest abortions. A State can thus transform what, when freely undertaken, is a wonder into what, when forced, may be a nightmare. Some women, especially women of means, will find ways around the State's assertion of power. Others — those without money or childcare or the ability to take time off from work—will not be so fortunate. Maybe they will try an unsafe method of abortion, and come to physical harm, or even die. Maybe they will undergo pregnancy and have a child, but at significant personal or familial cost. At the least, they will incur the cost of losing control of their lives. The Constitution will, today's majority holds, provide no shield, despite its guarantees of liberty and equality for all.

And no one should be confident that this majority is done with its work. The right *Roe* and *Casey* recognized does not stand alone. To the contrary, the Court has linked it for decades to other settled freedoms involving bodily integrity, familial relationships, and procreation. Most obviously, the right to terminate a pregnancy arose straight out of the right to purchase and use contraception. In turn, those rights led, more recently, to rights of same-sex intimacy and marriage. They are all part of the same constitutional fabric, protecting autonomous decisionmaking over the most personal of life decisions. The majority (or to be more accurate, most of it) is eager to tell us today that nothing it does "cast[s] doubt on precedents that do not concern abortion." But how could that be? The lone rationale for what the majority does today is that the right to elect an abortion is not "deeply rooted in history": Not until *Roe*, the majority argues, did people think abortion fell within the Constitution's guarantee of liberty. The same could be said, though, of most of the rights the majority claims it is not tampering with. The majority could write just as long an opinion showing, for example, that until the mid-20th century, "there was no support in American law for a constitutional right to obtain [contraceptives]." So one of two things must be true. Either the majority does not really believe in its own reasoning. Or if it does, all rights that have no history stretching back to the mid-19th century are insecure. Either the mass of the majority's opinion is hypocrisy, or additional constitutional rights are under threat. It is one or the other.

One piece of evidence on that score seems especially salient: The majority's cavalier approach to overturning this Court's precedents. *Stare decisis* is the Latin phrase for a foundation stone of the rule of law: that things decided should stay decided unless there is a very good reason for change. It is a doctrine of judicial modesty and humility. Those qualities are not evident in today's opinion. The majority has no good reason for the upheaval in law and society it sets off. *Roe* and *Casey* have been the law of the land for decades, shaping women's expectations of their choices when an unplanned pregnancy occurs. Women have relied on the availability of abortion both in structuring their relationships and in planning their lives. The legal framework *Roe* and *Casey* developed to balance the competing interests in this sphere has proved workable in courts across the country. No recent developments, in either law or fact, have eroded or cast doubt on those precedents. Nothing, in short, has changed. Indeed, the Court in *Casey* already found all of that to be true. *Casey* is a precedent about precedent. It reviewed the same arguments made here in support of overruling *Roe*, and it found that doing so was not warranted. The Court reverses course today for one reason and one reason only: because the composition of this Court has changed.

Stare decisis, this Court has often said, "contributes to the actual and perceived integrity of the judicial process" by ensuring that decisions are "founded in the law rather than in the proclivities of individuals." Today, the proclivities of individuals rule. The Court departs from its obligation to faithfully and impartially apply the law. We dissent. . . .

NOTES

1. Equal Protection: The Road Not Taken. The late Justice Ruth Bader Ginsburg famously argued that the right to abortion would have been on a much stronger constitutional footing had the Court framed abortion bans as a gender discrimination issue. *See, e.g.*, Ginsburg, Some Thoughts on Autonomy and Equality in Relation to *Roe v. Wade*, 63 N.C. L. Rev. 375, 386 (1985). Justice Alito's opinion considered and rejected this argument:

> Neither *Roe* nor *Casey* saw fit to invoke [the abortion-as-sex-discrimination theory], and it is squarely foreclosed by our precedents, which establish that a State's regulation of abortion is not a sex-based classification and is thus not subject to the "heightened scrutiny" that applies to such classifications. The regulation of a medical procedure that only one sex can undergo does not trigger heightened constitutional scrutiny unless the regulation is a "mere pretex[t] designed to effect an invidious discrimination against members of one sex or the other." And as the Court has stated, the "goal of preventing abortion" does not constitute "invidiously discriminatory animus" against women. Accordingly, laws regulating or prohibiting abortion are not subject to heightened scrutiny. Rather, they are governed by the same standard of review as other health and safety measures.

Is this a sufficient response to the argument that abortion affects women uniquely? How would one prove "discriminatory animus"?

2. History, Tradition, and the Future of Substantive Due Process. The *Dobbs* Court says it looks to history and tradition when asked to recognize an unenumerated right. Does that mean that the majority will regard, as the dissent alleges, all potential unenumerated rights to be only those that may have existed in 1868, when the Fourteenth Amendment was ratified? How well-recognized in history and tradition does the right have to be? Note that several cases in the 2021 Term looked to history and tradition in describing the scope of other rights; notably, the right to keep and bear arms and the free exercise rights. Does this suggest a broader methodological project is afoot?

3. The First Step in a Long March? The dissent warns that the overruling of *Roe* and *Casey* are simply the first step in the dismantling of decisions that came before, like *Griswold*, and those that came after, such as *Lawrence v. Texas* or *Obergefell*. The majority opinion states those issues are different; Justice Kavanaugh emphasized that point in his concurrence. By contrast, Justice

Thomas signals his readiness to revisit—and presumably overrule—a host of other substantive due process cases. As you read those cases, ask yourself whether there is a principled way to distinguish those cases from *Dobbs*.

4. *Stare Decisis* and the "Moment of Repose." In a famous Supreme Court case, the petitioners asked the Court to overrule a case that was a half century old; arguably a good number of states and private individuals had relied on that case in ordering public and private institutions and their daily lives. At oral argument, the lawyer for the respondent said, "[s]omewhere, some time, to every principle there comes a moment of repose when it has been so often pronounced, so confidently relied upon, so long continued, that it passes the limit of judicial discretion and disturbance." The speaker was John W. Davis, then a well-respected Supreme Court litigator; his client was the state of South Carolina. The case was one of the companion cases in *Brown v. Board of Education* and the principle he was referring to was that of "separate-but-equal." Does the dissent make a similar "moment of repose" argument in its criticism of the majority for abandoning *stare decisis*? How effective is the majority's response that *Roe* was wrong the day it was decided, and that *Casey* never really came to grips with *Roe*'s analytical shortcomings? Should it make a difference that the principle of separate but equal had been systematically undermined in a series of cases brought by the NCAA Legal Defense Fund that allowed its lawyers to argue, in *Brown*, that separate could *never* be equal. For an account of those cases, see Chapter 8.C.3.a. *infra*.

5. Abortion Regulation and the Rational Basis Test. Justice Alito is clear that the new standard of review is the rational basis test, and then he lists a number of legitimate state interests that states have in regulating abortion. Can you think of a regulation that might violate the rational basis test as articulated by the majority opinion? Do you think that the version of the test Justice Alito describes is the traditional, deferential rational basis test or is there room for the application of "rational basis with bite" applied in cases like *Lawrence v. Texas* or the equal protection cases discussed in Chapter 8.B.2. *infra*?

6. Sophistry's Choice. Chief Justice Roberts voted to uphold Mississippi's law, but leave *Roe* and *Casey* partially in tact. Does this just postpone the inevitable, as Justice Alito alleged? Or given the tumult that accompanied the decision, would it have allowed time for the public to acclimate itself to the direction the majority seemed to be taking? Is that unprincipled decisionmaking or is it simply a prudent exercise of judicial restraint?

7. Abortion Rights as State Constitutional Rights. Expect plaintiffs in states with restrictive abortion laws to bring state constitutional law claims. Some state constitutions have explicit clauses recognizing a right to privacy that could serve as a basis for a legal challenge.

8. Federal Abortion Statutes. Both pro-life and pro-choice activist have long sought to enshrine their preferred position in federal law that would preempt contrary state laws. What Article I, § 8 power would provide the basis for either piece of legislation?

9. Abortion, Privileges and Immunities, and the Dormant Commerce Clause. Could states punish women who traveled out of state to obtain an abortion or abortifacients? Could they ban the importation of abortifacients? Could women be criminally punished for having an out-of-state abortion? When you think about those questions, you might review the material covered in Chapter 4.

Chapter 7

Economic Rights: The Takings and Contracts Clauses

A. The Takings Clause

Page 570: Insert new paragraph before the last full paragraph:

The question of *when* a taking has occurred created difficulties for some claimants. In 1985, the Court decided Williamson County Regional Planning Comm'n v. Hamilton Bank of Johnson City, 473 U.S. 172, in which it held that a property owner could not bring a takings claim in federal court until that claim had been denied by state court; such a federal claim in the absence of a state denial would not be ripe. Twenty years later, however, the Court held that a state denial of a claim for just compensation would have preclusive effect in a subsequent federal suit. San Remo Hotel, L.P. v. City and County of San Francisco, 545 U.S. 323 (2005). This "preclusion trap" created a Catch-22 for plaintiffs: they could not get into federal court prior to a state court ruling; if their claim was denied, the claim would be barred in federal court. In Knick v. Township of Scott, 139 S. Ct. 2161 (2019), the Court abandoned the state litigation requirement. "A property owner has an actionable Fifth Amendment takings claim," the Court wrote, "when the government takes his property without paying for it."

Page 599: Insert new paragraph following the last full paragraph in note b:

The Court reaffirmed *Loretto* and *Causby* in Cedar Point Nursery v. Hassid, 141 S. Ct. 2063 (2021). California's labor regulations gave labor unions a "right to take access" to agricultural employers in order to organize workers. The access was mandated for up to three hours a day, 120 days per year. One employer sued, claiming that the regulation was a taking. The Court agreed. "Government action," Chief Justice Roberts wrote, "is no less a physical taking because it arises from a regulation." He continued, "[t]he access regulation appropriates a right to invade the growers' property and therefore constitutes a *per se* physical taking. . . . [T]he regulation appropriates for the enjoyment of third parties' the owners' right to exclude." Three dissenting justices led by Justice Breyer characterized the regulation not as a physical appropriation, but rather as a *regulation* of the employer's property rights subject to the more deferential balancing test of Penn Central Transportation Co. v. New York, 438 U.S. 104 (1983). That test is discussed in the next section.

Chapter 8

Equal Protection

F.   Fundamental Rights: Strict Scrutiny Redux

4.   Voting: Gerrymanders

Page 807: Replace notes 1 and 2 with the following note:

1. Subsequent Developments. In the years following *Bandemer*, standards for measuring how much partisan influence in redistricting was "too much" proved elusive. In Vieth v. Jubelirer, 541 U.S. 267 (2004), a plurality of four justices would have overturned *Bandemer* and declared the question of the validity of political gerrymanders to be a nonjusticiable political question. Following the 2000 census, Pennsylvania's legislature, dominated by Republicans, adopted a congressional redistricting plan, which was attacked as a violation of equal protection because the plan "ignored all traditional redistricting criteria . . . solely for the sake of partisan advantage." Justice Scalia, joined by Chief Justice Rehnquist and Justices O'Connor and Thomas, concluded that there are "no judicially discernible and manageable standards for adjudicating political gerrymandering claims."

Although "intentional discrimination against an identifiable political group" is easy enough to prove, the plurality thought that judicial assessment of proof of "an actual discriminatory effect on that group" was well-nigh impossible. Next, the plurality rejected a proposed test focusing on "predominant intent" and specific effect. The problem with the "predominant intent" prong of the test was the near impossibility of proving that "partisan advantage was the predominant motivation" for the district boundaries. The "effects prong" of the proposed test would have required proof of (1) systematic "packing" and "cracking" of "the rival party's voters," and (2) a totality of circumstances establishing that the gerrymander "'thwart[s] the plaintiffs' ability to translate a majority of votes into a majority of seats.'" The plurality thought this prong was neither discernible nor manageable. First, because "[p]olitical affiliation" is not an immutable characteristic, [it is] impossible to assess the effects of partisan gerrymandering, to fashion a standard for evaluating a violation, and finally to craft a remedy." Second, the proposed effects standard was not "judicially discernible in the sense of being relevant to some constitutional violation" because it "rests upon the principle that [political] groups have a right to proportional representation, [and] the Constitution contains no such principle." Finally, the proposed standard was "not judicially manageable" because it is virtually impossible to "identify a majority party" with certainty, and even more difficult to ensure that the "majority" party wins a majority of seats, if only because voters remain maddeningly independent of party affiliation when it comes time to cast ballots.

Justices Stevens and Kennedy concurred in the judgment. Justice Kennedy concluded that the claim presented in *Vieth* was nonjusticiable, but was unwilling to conclude that all such claims are nonjusticiable: "I would not foreclose all possibility of judicial relief if some limited and precise rationale were found to correct an established violation of the Constitution in some redistricting cases." Justice Stevens contended that political gerrymandering claims at the individual district level are justiciable. He likened political gerrymanders to racial gerrymanders, an analogy disputed by the plurality: "[S]etting out to segregate voters by race is unlawful[;] setting out to segregate them by political affiliation is lawful. . . . A purpose to discriminate on the basis of race receives the strictest scrutiny under the Equal Protection Clause, while a similar purpose to discriminate on the basis of politics does not."

Justice Souter, joined by Justice Ginsburg, dissented, concluding that the case was justiciable and proposing a new, complicated, multi-factor test to identify such an "extremity of unfairness" in gerrymandering that equal protection is violated, a goal that the plurality derided as "utterly unhelpful" because it does not illuminate "the precise constitutional deprivation [the] test is designed to identify and prevent." Justice Breyer also dissented, contending that statewide political gerrymanders are justiciable when "the *unjustified* use of political factors . . . entrench a minority in power." The plurality tartly dismissed this approach by noting that it requires the judiciary to "assess whether a group (somehow defined) has achieved a level of political power (somehow defined) commensurate with that to which they would be entitled absent *unjustified* political machinations (whatever that means)."

After the 2000 census, Texas gained two House seats, but because the legislature could not agree on a redistricting plan, a federal court devised a plan that did not disturb the disproportionate hold of Democrats on its House delegation (17 D, 15 R), even though Republicans garnered 59 percent of the statewide vote. By 2003, however, Republicans controlled both houses of the Texas legislature as well as the governorship, and they used their political muscle to enact a new redistricting plan that, in 2004, resulted in 58 percent of the statewide vote favoring Republicans, and a Texas House delegation of 21 Republicans and 11 Democrats.

Various groups and voters allied with Democratic interests brought suit, contending that the 2003 plan was an unconstitutional political gerrymander. In League of United Latin American Citizens v. Perry, 548 U.S. 399 (2006), the Court rejected the political gerrymander claim. The Court did not revisit the justiciability issue debated in *Vieth*, but confined itself to examination of whether the "claims offer the Court a manageable, reliable measure of fairness for determining whether a partisan gerrymander violates the Constitution." A plurality consisting of Justice Kennedy, Chief Justice Roberts, and Justice Alito concluded that a mid-decade redistricting was valid even though there was evidence that the Texas legislature was motivated primarily but not exclusively by the desire to obtain partisan advantage. However, it was uncontested that some Democratic desires for district lines were honored.

> . . . The text and structure of the Constitution and our case law indicate there is nothing inherently suspect about a legislature's decision to replace mid-decade a court-ordered plan with one of its own. [Appellants] would leave untouched the 1991 Texas redistricting, which entrenched [the Democratic Party,] a party on the verge of minority status, while striking down the 2003 redistricting plan, which resulted in the majority Republican Party capturing a larger share of the seats. [While] there is no constitutional requirement of proportional representation, . . . a congressional plan that more closely reflects the distribution of state party power seems a less likely vehicle for partisan discrimination than one that entrenches an electoral minority. . . .

Justice Stevens, joined by Justice Breyer, dissented:

> Because a desire to minimize the strength of Texas Democrats was the sole motivation for the adoption of [the challenged plan, it] cannot withstand constitutional scrutiny. . . . [A]lthough the Constitution places no *per se* ban on midcycle redistricting, a legislature's decision to redistrict in the middle of the census cycle, when the legislature is under no legal obligation to do so, . . . raises a fair inference that partisan machinations played a major role in the map-drawing process.

Chief Justice Roberts, joined by Justice Alito, took no position on the question of whether a political gerrymander constituted a justiciable controversy because that issue had not been argued to the Court. Justice Scalia and Justice Thomas concurred in the judgment with respect to the mid-decade redistricting but dissented as to the justiciability of the claim. They reiterated their view, expressed in *Vieth*, that political gerrymanders present nonjusticiable political questions.

The Court was again asked to rule on the constitutionality of partisan gerrymandering in Gill v. Whitford, 138 S. Ct. 1916 (2016); once again, the Court declined, this time on the grounds that the plaintiffs lacked standing to bring their claim. The plaintiffs argued that their injury not only occurred in their individual districts but also "extend[ed] . . . to the statewide harm to their interest 'in their collective representation in the legislature,' and in influencing the legislature's overall 'composition and policymaking.' " The Court found that insufficient to maintain standing: "A citizen's interest in the overall composition of the legislature is embodied in his right to vote for his representative. And the citizen's abstract interest in policies adopted by the legislature on the facts here is a nonjusticiable 'general interest common to all members of the public.' " The Court noted that

> [I]t appears that not a single plaintiff sought to prove that he or she lives in a cracked or packed district. They instead rested their case at trial—and their arguments before this Court—on their theory of statewide injury to Wisconsin Democrats . . . .

Instead of directing the dismissal of the plaintiffs' case for want of jurisdiction, however, the Court remanded it to the district court "so that the plaintiffs may have an opportunity to prove concrete and particularized injuries using evidence . . . that would tend to demonstrate a burden on their individual votes."

Justice Kagan, in a concurring opinion joined by Justices Ginsburg, Breyer, and Sotomayor went further, suggesting precisely how the plaintiffs' might secure a statewide remedy as a result of individually establishing that their districts had been packed or cracked.

> . . . The Court properly remands this case to the District Court "so that the plaintiffs may have an opportunity" to "demonstrate a burden on their individual votes." That means the plaintiffs—both the four who initially made those assertions and any others (current or newly joined)—now can introduce evidence that their individual districts were packed or cracked. And if the plaintiffs' more general charges have a basis in fact, that evidence may well be at hand. Recall that the plaintiffs here alleged—and the District Court found—that a unified Republican government set out to ensure that Republicans would control as many State Assembly seats as possible over a decade (five consecutive election cycles). To that end, the government allegedly packed and cracked Democrats throughout the State, not just in a particular district . . . or region. Assuming that is true, the plaintiffs should have a mass of packing and cracking proof, which they can now also present in district-by-district form to support their standing. In other words, a plaintiff residing in each affected district can show, through an alternative map or other evidence, that packing or cracking indeed occurred there. And if (or to the extent) that test is met, the court can proceed to decide all distinctive merits issues and award appropriate remedies.
>
> When the court addresses those merits questions, it can consider statewide (as well as local) evidence. Of course, the court below and others like it are currently debating, without guidance from this Court, what elements make up a vote dilution claim in the partisan gerrymandering context. But assume that the plaintiffs must prove illicit partisan intent—a purpose to dilute Democrats' votes in drawing district lines. The plaintiffs could then offer evidence about the mapmakers' goals in formulating the entire statewide map (which would predictably carry down to individual districting decisions). So, for example, the plaintiffs here introduced proof that the mapmakers looked to partisan voting data when drawing districts throughout the State—and that they graded draft maps according to the amount of advantage those maps conferred on Republicans. This Court has explicitly recognized the relevance of such statewide evidence in addressing racial gerrymandering claims of a district-specific nature. "Voters," we held, "of course[] can present statewide evidence in order to prove racial gerrymandering in a particular district."

And in particular, "[s]uch evidence is perfectly relevant" to showing that mapmakers had an invidious "motive" in drawing the lines of "multiple districts in the State." The same should be true for partisan gerrymandering.

Similarly, cases like this one might warrant a statewide remedy. Suppose that mapmakers pack or crack a critical mass of State Assembly districts all across the State to elect as many Republican politicians as possible. And suppose plaintiffs residing in those districts prevail in a suit challenging that gerrymander on a vote dilution theory. The plaintiffs might then receive exactly the relief sought in this case. To be sure, remedying each plaintiff's vote dilution injury "requires revising only such districts as are necessary to reshape [that plaintiff's] district—so that the [plaintiff] may be unpacked or uncracked, as the case may be." But with enough plaintiffs joined together—attacking all the packed and cracked districts in a statewide gerrymander—those obligatory revisions could amount to a wholesale restructuring of the State's districting plan. The Court recognizes as much. It states that a proper remedy in a vote dilution case "does not necessarily require restructuring all of the State's legislative districts." Not necessarily—but possibly. It all depends on how much redistricting is needed to cure all the packing and cracking that the mapmakers have done.

She further suggested that the plaintiffs allege that "partisan gerrymanders . . . infringe the First Amendment rights of association held by parties, other political organizations, and their members," noting that such an "associational claim would occasion a different standing inquiry than the one in the Court's opinion."

In a related case in which Republican voters claimed that a congressional district was gerrymandered in order to retaliate against them for their political views, the Court upheld the decision of a three-judge panel not to issue a preliminary injunction. "Even if we assume—contrary to the findings of the District Court—that plaintiffs were likely to succeed on the merits of their claims, the balance of equities and the public interest tilted against their request for a preliminary injunction." Benisek v. Lamone, 138 S. Ct. 1932 (2018).

Finally, in Rucho v. Common Cause, 139 S. Ct. 2484 (2019), the Court pulled the plug on partisan gerrymandering cases, holding that they present nonjusticiable political questions. This case arose out of a suit brought in North Carolina alleging that the state's congressional districts were drawn to advantage Republicans and harm Democrats. In a 5-4 decision, Chief Justice Roberts wrote:

Excessive partisanship in districting leads to results that reasonably seem unjust. But the fact that such gerrymandering is "incompatible with democratic principles," does not mean that the solution lies with the federal judiciary. We conclude that partisan gerrymandering claims present political questions beyond the reach of the federal courts. Federal judges have no license to reallocate political power between the two major political parties, with no plausible grant of authority in the Constitution, and no legal standards to limit and direct their decisions. "[J]udicial action must be governed by *standard*, by *rule*," and must be "principled, rational, and based upon reasoned distinctions" found in the Constitution or laws. Judicial review of partisan gerrymandering does not meet those basic requirements.

He observed that under the Elections Clause of the Constitution, which empowers states to set the time, place, and manner of electing federal representatives, Congress retains authority to alter those, except for where senators are chosen. He also noted that—as to state legislatures—voters have had success challenging redistricting in state courts.

Chapter 9

Free Expression of Ideas

A. Overview of Free Expression

2. The Distinction Between Content-Based Regulation and Content-Neutral Regulation

Page 839: Insert the following note before section B.:

Austin v. Reagan National Advertising of Austin, LLC, ___ *S. Ct.* ____ *(2022).* Members of the Court sparred over *Reed*'s holding recently in a case involving regulation of outdoor advertising. Like many cities, Austin, Texas regulates "off-premises" advertising—signs advertising products and services not located on the site where the sign was installed. New construction of off-premises signs was prohibited with existing advertising grandfathered in, but with the proviso that they couldn't be altered in ways that would increase their nonconformity, such as digitization. Outdoor advertising companies sued, claiming that the distinction between on-premises and off-premises advertising violated the First Amendment citing *Reed* among other cases.

The Court rejected that argument and found the regulation to be content-neutral. Justice Sotomayor wrote:

> Unlike the sign code at issue in *Reed* . . . the City's provisions at issue here do not single out any topic or subject matter for differential treatment. A sign's substantive message itself is irrelevant to the application of the provisions; there are no content-discriminatory classifications for political messages, ideological messages, or directional messages concerning specific events, including those sponsored by religious and nonprofit organizations.

The majority remanded the case for application of intermediate scrutiny. Justice Alito concurred in the judgment, but objected to the majority's categorical statement that all on/off-premises distinctions were content-neutral; he argued that in some cases strict scrutiny would be appropriate.

Justice Thomas, writing for himself and Justices Gorsuch and Barrett dissented. He argued that the majority had diluted *Reed* and that the distinction *was* content-based because "off-premise" advertisements included those which directed people elsewhere.

Much like in *Reed*, that an Austin official applying the sign code must know where the sign is does not negate the fact that he also must know what the sign says. Take, for instance, a sign outside a Catholic bookstore. If the sign says, "Visit the Holy Land," it is likely an off-premises sign because it conveys a message directing people elsewhere (unless the name of the bookstore is "Holy Land Books"). But if the sign instead says, "Buy More Books," it is likely a permissible on-premises sign (unless the sign also contains the address of another bookstore across town).

Which side has the better of the argument?

B.   Content-Based Regulations of Speech

5.   Offensive Speech

a. The General Rule

Page 896: Insert the following note before section b.:

NOTE

The Lanham Act had a similar provision that instructed the PTO to refuse registration of trademarks that were "scandalous" or "immoral." When Erik Brunetti attempted to trademark the name of his line of clothing, FUCT—it reportedly stands for "Friends U Can't Trust"—his application was denied. Noting the Court's decision in *Tam* and the "core postulate of free speech law" on which the case was based—that "[t]he government may not discriminate against speech based on the ideas or opinions it conveys"— the Court concluded that the restrictions were viewpoint-based and thus unconstitutional. Iancu v. Brunetti, 139 S. Ct. 2294 (2019). The Court declined the government's invitation to read the language to encompass only "lewd, sexually explicit, or profane marks." The government's argument was appealing—at least as applied to the prohibition on "scandalous" marks—to several Justices who filed concurring opinions.

D.   Regulation of Speech When the Government is Both Sovereign and Proprietor

2.   Public Education

Page 1021: Insert the following after note 4:

MAHANOY AREA SCHOOL DISTRICT v. B.L.
Supreme Court of the United States
141 S. Ct. 2038 (2021)

JUSTICE BREYER delivered the opinion of the Court. . . .

I. A. B. L. . . . was a student at Mahanoy Area High School, a public school in Mahanoy City, Pennsylvania. At the end of her freshman year, B. L. tried out for a position on the school's varsity cheerleading squad and for right fielder on a private softball team. She did not make the varsity cheerleading team or get her preferred softball position, but she was offered a spot on the cheerleading squad's junior varsity team. B. L. did not accept the coach's decision with good grace, particularly because the squad coaches had placed an entering freshman on the varsity team.

That weekend, B. L. and a friend visited the Cocoa Hut, a local convenience store. There, B. L. used her smartphone to post two photos on Snapchat, a social media application that allows users to post photos and videos that disappear after a set period of time. B. L. posted the images to her Snapchat "story," a feature of the application that allows any person in the user's "friend" group (B. L. had about 250 "friends") to view the images for a 24 hour period.

The first image B. L. posted showed B. L. and a friend with middle fingers raised; it bore the caption: "Fuck school fuck softball fuck cheer fuck everything." The second image was blank but for a caption, which read: "Love how me and [another student] get told we need a year of jv before we make varsity but tha[t] doesn't matter to anyone else?" The caption also contained an upside-down smiley-face emoji.

B. L.'s Snapchat "friends" included other Mahanoy Area High School students, some of whom also belonged to the cheerleading squad. At least one of them, using a separate cellphone, took pictures of B. L.'s posts and shared them with other members of the cheerleading squad. One of the students who received these photos showed them to her mother (who was a cheerleading squad coach), and the images spread. That week, several cheerleaders and other students approached the cheerleading coaches "visibly upset" about B. L.'s posts. Questions about the posts persisted during an Algebra class taught by one of the two coaches.

After discussing the matter with the school principal, the coaches decided that because the posts used profanity in connection with a school extracurricular activity, they violated team and school rules. As a result, the coaches suspended B. L. from the junior varsity cheerleading squad for the upcoming year. B. L.'s subsequent apologies did not move school officials. The school's athletic director, principal, superintendent, and school board, all affirmed B. L.'s suspension from the team. In response, B. L., together with her parents, filed this lawsuit in Federal District Court.

B. [B.L. won in the lower courts. The district court found that her posts had not been disruptive. The Third Circuit affirmed the decision, and went farther, holding that schools could not discipline students for pure speech that occurs off-campus.]

II. We have made clear that students do not "shed their constitutional rights to freedom of speech or expression," even "at the school house gate." But we have also made clear that courts must apply the First Amendment "in light of the special characteristics of the school environment." One such characteristic, which we have stressed, is the fact that schools at times stand *in loco parentis, i.e.,* in the place of parents.

This Court has previously outlined three specific categories of student speech that schools may regulate in certain circumstances: (1) "indecent," "lewd," or "vulgar" speech uttered during a school assembly on school grounds; (2) speech, uttered during a class trip, that promotes "illegal drug use;" and (3) speech that others may reasonably perceive as "bear[ing] the imprimatur of the school," such as that appearing in a school-sponsored newspaper.

Finally, in *Tinker,* we said schools have a special interest in regulating speech that "materially disrupts classwork or involves substantial disorder or invasion of the rights of others." These special characteristics call for special leeway when schools regulate speech that occurs under its supervision.

Unlike the Third Circuit, we do not believe the special characteristics that give schools additional license to regulate student speech always disappear when a school regulates speech that takes place off campus. The school's regulatory interests remain significant in some off-campus circumstances. . . . These include serious or severe bullying or harassment targeting particular individuals; threats aimed at teachers or other students; the failure to follow rules concerning lessons, the writing of papers, the use of computers, or participation in other online school activities; and breaches of school security devices, including material maintained within school computers.

. . . And it may be that speech related to extracurricular activities, such as team sports, would also receive special treatment under B. L.'s proposed rule.

We are uncertain as to the length or content of any such list of appropriate exceptions or carveouts to the Third Circuit majority's rule . . . Thus, we do not now set forth a broad, highly general First Amendment rule stating just what counts as "off campus" speech and whether or how ordinary First Amendment standards must give way off campus to a school's special need to prevent, *e.g.,* substantial disruption of learning-related activities or the protection of those who make up a school community.

We can, however, mention three features of off-campus speech that often, even if not always, distinguish schools' efforts to regulate that speech from their efforts to regulate on-campus speech. Those features diminish the strength of the unique educational characteristics that might call for special First Amendment leeway.

First, a school, in relation to off-campus speech, will rarely stand *in loco parentis*. . . . Geographically speaking, off-campus speech will normally fall within the zone of parental, rather than school-related, responsibility.

Second, from the student speaker's perspective, regulations of off-campus speech, when coupled with regulations of on-campus speech, include all the speech a student utters during the full 24-hour day. . . . When it comes to political or religious speech that occurs outside school or a school program or activity, the school will have a heavy burden to justify intervention.

Third, the school itself has an interest in protecting a student's unpopular expression, especially when the expression takes place off campus. America's public schools are the nurseries of democracy. Our representative democracy only works if we protect the "marketplace of ideas." This free exchange facilitates an informed public opinion, which, when transmitted to lawmakers, helps produce laws that reflect the People's will. That protection must include the protection of unpopular ideas, for popular ideas have less need for protection. . . .

. . . Taken together, these three features of much off-campus speech mean that the leeway the First Amendment grants to schools in light of their special characteristics is diminished. We leave for future cases to decide where, when, and how these features mean the speaker's off-campus location will make the critical difference. This case can, however, provide one example.

III. Consider B. L.'s speech. Putting aside the vulgar language, the listener would hear criticism, of the team, the team's coaches, and the school—in a word or two, criticism of the rules of a community of which B. L. forms a part. This criticism did not involve features that would place it outside the First Amendment's ordinary protection. B. L.'s posts, while crude, did not amount to fighting words. And while B. L. used vulgarity, her speech was not obscene as this Court has understood that term. To the contrary, B. L. uttered the kind of pure speech to which, were she an adult, the First Amendment would provide strong protection.

Consider too when, where, and how B. L. spoke. Her posts appeared outside of school hours from a location outside the school. She did not identify the school in her posts or target any member of the school community with vulgar or abusive language. B. L. also transmitted her speech through a personal cellphone, to an audience consisting of her private circle of Snapchat friends. These features of her speech, while risking transmission to the school itself, nonetheless . . . diminish the school's interest in punishing B. L.'s utterance.

But what about the school's interest, here primarily an interest in prohibiting students from using vulgar language to criticize a school team or its coaches—at least when that criticism might well be transmitted to other students, team members, coaches, and faculty? . . .

First, we consider the school's interest in teaching good manners and consequently in punishing the use of vulgar language aimed at part of the school community. The strength of this anti-vulgarity interest is weakened considerably by the fact that B. L. spoke outside the school on her own time.

B. L. spoke under circumstances where the school did not stand *in loco parentis*. And there is no reason to believe B. L.'s parents had delegated to school officials their own control of B. L.'s behavior at the Cocoa Hut. Moreover, the vulgarity in B. L.'s posts encompassed a message, an expression of B. L.'s irritation with, and criticism of, the school and cheerleading communities. Further, the school has presented no evidence of any general effort to prevent students from using vulgarity outside the classroom. Together, these facts convince us that the school's interest in teaching good manners is not sufficient, in this case, to overcome B. L.'s interest in free expression.

Second, the school argues that it was trying to prevent disruption, if not within the classroom, then within the bounds of a school-sponsored extracurricular activity. But we can find no evidence in the record of the sort of "substantial disruption" of a school activity or a threatened harm to the rights of others that might justify the school's action. Rather, the record shows that discussion of the matter took, at most, 5 to 10 minutes of an Algebra class "for just a couple of days" and that some members of the cheerleading team were "upset" about the content of B. L.'s Snapchats. . . . The alleged disturbance here does not meet *Tinker*'s demanding standard [of "substantial disruption."]

Third, the school presented some evidence that expresses (at least indirectly) a concern for team morale. One of the coaches testified that the school decided to suspend B. L., not because of any specific negative impact upon a particular member of the school community, but "based on the fact that there was negativity put out there that could impact students in the school." There is little else, however, that suggests any serious decline in team morale—to the point where it could create a substantial interference in, or disruption of, the school's efforts to maintain team cohesion. As we have previously said, simple "undifferentiated fear or apprehension . . . is not enough to overcome the right to freedom of expression."

It might be tempting to dismiss B. L.'s words as unworthy of the robust First Amendment protections discussed herein. But sometimes it is necessary to protect the superfluous in order to preserve the necessary.

* * *

Although we do not agree with the reasoning of the Third Circuit's panel majority, for the reasons expressed above, resembling those of the panel's concurring opinion, we nonetheless agree that the school violated B. L.'s First Amendment rights. The judgment of the Third Circuit is therefore affirmed.

JUSTICE ALITO, with whom JUSTICE GORSUCH joins, concurring.

II. I start with this threshold question: Why does the First Amendment ever allow the free-speech rights of public school students to be restricted to a greater extent than the rights of other juveniles who do not attend a public school? . . .

The only plausible answer that comes readily to mind is consent, either express or implied. The theory must be that by enrolling a child in a public school, parents consent on behalf of the child to the relinquishment of some of the child's free-speech rights. . . .

If *in loco parentis* is transplanted from Blackstone's England to the 21st century United States, what it amounts to is simply a doctrine of inferred parental consent to a public school's exercise of a degree of authority that is commensurate with the task that the parents ask the school to perform. Because public school students attend school for only part of the day and continue to live at home, the degree of authority conferred is obviously less than that delegated to the head of a late-18th century boarding school, but because public school students are taught outside the home, the authority conferred may be greater in at least some respects than that enjoyed by a tutor of Blackstone's time.

So how much authority to regulate speech do parents implicitly delegate when they enroll a child at a public school? The answer must be that parents are treated as having relinquished the measure of authority that the schools must be able to exercise in order to carry out their state-mandated educational mission, as well as the authority to perform any other functions to which parents expressly or implicitly agree — for example, by giving permission for a child to participate in an extracurricular activity or to go on a school trip. . . .

IV. A. A public school's regulation of off-premises student speech is a different matter. . . . In our society, parents, not the State, have the primary authority and duty to raise, educate, and form the character of their children. Parents do not implicitly relinquish all that authority when they send their children to a public school. . . .

B. The degree to which enrollment in a public school can be regarded as a delegation of authority over off-campus speech depends on the nature of the speech and the circumstances under which it occurs. [R]elevant lower court cases tend to fall into a few basic groups. And with respect to speech in each of these groups, the question that courts must ask is whether parents who enroll their children in a public school can reasonably be understood to have delegated to the school the authority to regulate the speech in question.

One category of off-premises student speech falls easily within the scope of the authority that parents implicitly or explicitly provide. This category includes speech that takes place during or as part of what amounts to a temporal or spatial extension of the regular school program, *e.g.,* online instruction at home, assigned essays or other homework, and transportation to and from school. Also included are statements made during other school activities in which students participate with their parents' consent, such as school trips, school sports and other extracurricular activities that may take place after regular school hours or

off school premises, and after-school programs for students who would otherwise be without adult supervision during that time. Abusive speech that occurs
while students are walking to and from school may also fall into this category on
the theory that it is school attendance that puts students on that route and in the
company of the fellow students who engage in the abuse. The imperatives that
justify the regulation of student speech while in school — the need for orderly
and effective instruction and student protection — apply more or less equally to
these off-premises activities. . . .

At the other end of the spectrum, there is a category of speech that is almost
always beyond the regulatory authority of a public school. This is student speech
that is not expressly and specifically directed at the school, school administrators, teachers, or fellow students and that addresses matters of public concern,
including sensitive subjects like politics, religion, and social relations. Speech on
such matters lies at the heart of the First Amendment's protection, and the connection between student speech in this category and the ability of a public school
to carry out its instructional program is tenuous.

If a school tried to regulate such speech, the most that it could claim is that
offensive off-premises speech on important matters may cause controversy and
recriminations among students and may thus disrupt instruction and good order
on school premises. But it is a "bedrock principle" that speech may not be sup-
pressed simply because it expresses ideas that are "offensive or disagreeable." It
is unreasonable to infer that parents who send a child to a public school thereby
authorize the school to take away such a critical right. . . .

This is true even if the student's off-premises speech on a matter of public
concern is intemperate and crude. When a student engages in oral or written
communication of this nature, the student is subject to whatever restraints the
student's parents impose, but the student enjoys the same First Amendment protection against government regulation as all other members of the public. . . .

Between these two extremes . . . lie the categories of off-premises student
speech that appear to have given rise to the most litigation. . . .

One group of cases involves perceived threats to school administrators,
teachers, other staff members, or students. Laws that apply to everyone prohibit
defined categories of threats, but schools have claimed that their duties demand
broader authority.

Another common category involves speech that criticizes or derides school
administrators, teachers, or other staff members. Schools may assert that parents
who send their children to a public school implicitly authorize the school to demand
that the child exhibit the respect that is required for orderly and effective instruction, but parents surely do not relinquish their children's ability to complain in an
appropriate manner about wrongdoing, dereliction, or even plain incompetence.

Perhaps the most difficult category involves criticism or hurtful remarks
about other students. Bullying and severe harassment are serious (and age-old)
problems, but these concepts are not easy to define with the precision required
for a regulation of speech.

V. The present case does not fall into any of these categories. Instead, it simply involves criticism (albeit in a crude manner) of the school and an extracurricular activity. Unflattering speech about a school or one of its programs is different from speech that criticizes or derides particular individuals, and for the reasons detailed by the Court . . . the school's justifications for punishing B. L.'s speech were weak. She sent the messages and image in question on her own time while at a local convenience store. They were transmitted via a medium that preserved the communication for only 24 hours, and she sent them to a select group of "friends." She did not send the messages to the school or to any administrator, teacher, or coach, and no member of the school staff would have even known about the messages if some of B. L.'s "friends" had not taken it upon themselves to spread the word.

The school did not claim that the messages caused any significant disruption of classes. The most it asserted along these lines was that they "upset" some students (including members of the cheerleading squad), caused students to ask some questions about the matter during an algebra class taught by a cheerleading coach, and put out "negativity . . . that could impact students in the school." The freedom of students to speak off-campus would not be worth much if it gave way in the face of such relatively minor complaints. . . .

As for the messages' effect on the morale of the cheerleading squad, the coach of a team sport may wish to take group cohesion and harmony into account in selecting members of the team, in assigning roles, and in allocating playing time, but it is self-evident that this authority has limits. . . . And here, the school did not simply take B. L.'s messages into account in deciding whether her attitude would make her effective in doing what cheerleaders are primarily expected to do: encouraging vocal fan support at the events where they appear. Instead, the school imposed punishment: suspension for a year from the cheerleading squad despite B. L.'s apologies.

There is, finally, the matter of B. L.'s language. There are parents who would not have been pleased with B. L.'s language and gesture, but whatever B. L.'s parents thought about what she did, it is not reasonable to infer that they gave the school the authority to regulate her choice of language when she was off school premises and not engaged in any school activity. And B. L.'s school does not claim that it possesses or makes any effort to exercise the authority to regulate the vocabulary and gestures of all its students 24 hours a day and 365 days a year.

. . . If today's decision teaches any lesson, it must be that the regulation of many types of off-premises student speech raises serious First Amendment concerns, and school officials should proceed cautiously before venturing into this territory.

Justice Thomas, dissenting.

B. L., a high school student, sent a profanity-laced message to hundreds of people, including classmates and teammates. The message included a picture of

B. L. raising her middle finger and captioned "F*** school" and "f*** cheer." This message was juxtaposed with another, which explained that B. L. was frustrated that she failed to make the varsity cheerleading squad. The cheerleading coach responded by disciplining B. L.

The Court overrides that decision — without even mentioning the 150 years of history supporting the coach. Using broad brushstrokes, the majority outlines the scope of school authority. When students are on campus, the majority says, schools have authority *in loco parentis* — that is, as substitutes of parents — to discipline speech and conduct. Off campus, the authority of schools is somewhat less. At that level of generality, I agree. But the majority omits important detail. What authority does a school have when it operates *in loco parentis*? How much less authority do schools have over off-campus speech and conduct? And how does a court decide if speech is on or off campus?

Disregarding these important issues, the majority simply posits three vague considerations and reaches an outcome. A more searching review reveals that schools historically could discipline students in circumstances like those presented here. Because the majority does not attempt to explain why we should not apply this historical rule and does not attempt to tether its approach to anything stable, I respectfully dissent. . . .

NOTES AND PROBLEM

1. Clear as Mud? Can you articulate the standard of review for off-campus speech? The Third Circuit had proclaimed a hard-edged rule: if it is pure speech and it occurs off campus, the school may not discipline a student for it. Why did the majority reject that clear and relatively easy-to-apply rule in favor of the less well-defined standards in Justice Breyer's opinion? Do you think lower courts will find this decision helpful in resolving future cases? The literature on legal rules versus legal standards is vast; both have advantages and disadvantages. For a summary discussion, see Frederick Schauer, Thinking Like a Lawyer 188-202 (2009).

2. Problem. A video on social media surfaces where two white teens have filmed themselves singing along to a popular song that makes free use of racial epithets. The students themselves use the same epithet to refer to each other. Their use of the epithet was not directed toward any member of a minority group nor was it used as a term of disparagement. The video was filmed at one of the student's house over a weekend. The video goes viral and receives extensive news coverage. There are protests outside the school and some minority students stage a walkout, demanding that the students who made the video be expelled. Could the school discipline the students in this case without violating the First Amendment?

3. Public Employment

Page 1033: Insert new note 2.:

2. Prayer as Private Speech. Kennedy v. Bremerton School District, 2022 WL 2295034 involved a head football coach who made it a practice to pray alone mid-field after games. For seven years he did this without anyone complaining. In addition, he would make pre-game motivational speeches that incorporated religious themes and continued the practice, which pre-dated him, of pregame or postgame prayer with players. Occasionally players — both from his team and the opposing team — would join him for his post-game, mid-field prayer. In September, 2015, the school district instructed Kennedy to avoid inspirational talks that alluded to religion and the supervision or encouragement of student prayer. His personal prayers, the letter continued, should be "nondemonstrative" in order to avoid the appearance of endorsement of religion by a public school employee. He briefly ceased his mid-field prayer, but resumed the practice in October, 2015. He informed the school district of this, but said that he would do this only after players and others had departed. Unwilling to pray privately, Kennedy continued to pray mid-field. In late October, he was put on administrative leave; and despite have received positive evaluations since his hiring, he received a poor evaluation in November, 2015 and did not return for thee next season. Kennedy sued in federal court, claiming the school district had violated his free speech and free exercise rights. In the portion of the opinion dealing with Kennedy's free speech claim, the Court acknowledged that as a public employee, the *Pickering-Garcetti* doctrine was applicable. The threshold question, then, was whether he was speaking pursuant to his official duties or as a private citizen on a matter of public concern. The majority wrote:

> Our cases offer some helpful guidance for resolving this question. In *Garcetti*, the Court concluded that a prosecutor's internal memorandum to a supervisor was made "pursuant to [his] official duties," and thus ineligible for First Amendment protection. In reaching this conclusion, the Court relied on the fact that the prosecutor's speech "fulfill[ed] a responsibility to advise his supervisor about how best to proceed with a pending case." In other words, the prosecutor's memorandum was government speech because it was speech the government "itself ha[d] commissioned or created" and speech the employee was expected to deliver in the course of carrying out his job.
>
> By contrast, in *Lane* a public employer sought to terminate an employee after he testified at a criminal trial about matters involving his government employment. The Court held that the employee's speech was protected by the First Amendment. In doing so, the Court held that the fact the speech touched on matters related to public employment was not enough to render it government speech. Instead, the Court explained, the "critical question . . . is whether the speech at issue is itself ordinarily within the scope of an employee's duties." It is an inquiry this Court has said should be undertaken "practical[ly]," rather than with a blinkered focus on the terms of some formal and capacious written job description. To proceed otherwise

would be to allow public employers to use "excessively broad job descriptions" to subvert the Constitution's protections.

Applying these lessons here, it seems clear to us that Mr. Kennedy has demonstrated that his speech was private speech, not government speech. When Mr. Kennedy uttered the three prayers that resulted in his suspension, he was not engaged in speech "ordinarily within the scope" of his duties as a coach. He did not speak pursuant to government policy. He was not seeking to convey a government-created message. He was not instructing players, discussing strategy, encouraging better on-field performance, or engaged in any other speech the District paid him to produce as a coach. Simply put: Mr. Kennedy's prayers did not "ow[e their] existence" to Mr. Kennedy's responsibilities as a public employee.

The timing and circumstances of Mr. Kennedy's prayers confirm the point. During the postgame period when these prayers occurred, coaches were free to attend briefly to personal matters — everything from checking sports scores on their phones to greeting friends and family in the stands. We find it unlikely that Mr. Kennedy was fulfilling a responsibility imposed by his employment by praying during a period in which the District has acknowledged that its coaching staff was free to engage in all manner of private speech. That Mr. Kennedy offered his prayers when students were engaged in other activities like singing the school fight song further suggests that those prayers were not delivered as an address to the team, but instead in his capacity as a private citizen. Nor is it dispositive that Mr. Kennedy's prayers took place "within the office" environment — here, on the field of play. Instead, what matters is whether Mr. Kennedy offered his prayers while acting within the scope of his duties as a coach. And taken together, both the substance of Mr. Kennedy's speech and the circumstances surrounding it point to the conclusion that he did not.

In her dissent, Justice Sotomayor thought that even if he was speaking as a private citizen, the school district had adequate reason to restrict his speech.

[T]he District has a strong argument that Kennedy's speech, formally integrated into the center of a District event, was speech in his official capacity as an employee that is not entitled to First Amendment protections at all. It is unnecessary to resolve this question, however, because, even assuming that Kennedy's speech was in his capacity as a private citizen, the District's responsibilities under the Establishment Clause provided "adequate justification" for restricting it.

Similarly, Kennedy's free exercise claim must be considered in light of the fact that he is a school official and, as such, his participation in religious exercise can create Establishment Clause conflicts. Accordingly, his right to pray at any time and in any manner he wishes while exercising his professional duties is not absolute. As the Court explains, the parties agree (and I therefore assume) that for the purposes of Kennedy's claim, the burden is on the District to establish that its policy prohibiting Kennedy's public prayers was the least restrictive means of furthering a compelling state interest.

Here, the District's directive prohibiting Kennedy's demonstrative speech at the 50-yard line was narrowly tailored to avoid an Establishment Clause violation. The District's suspension of Kennedy followed a long history. The last three games proved that Kennedy did not intend to pray silently, but to thrust the District into incorporating a religious ceremony into its events, as he invited others to join his prayer and anticipated in his communications with the District that students would want to join as well. Notably, the District repeatedly sought to work with Kennedy to develop an accommodation to permit him to engage in religious exercise during or after his game-related responsibilities. Kennedy, however, ultimately refused to respond to the District's suggestions and declined to communicate with the District, except through media appearances.

The Court's ruling on Kennedy's free exercise claim can be found in Chapter 10.B. *infra.*

4.   Public Sponsorship of Speech

Page 1045: Insert the following paragraph before "Matal v. Tam".*:*

In a follow up case, the Supreme Court held that the Alliance for Open Society International's foreign subsidiaries operating abroad had no First Amendment rights that could be violated by the Leadership Act. Agency for International Development v. Alliance for Open Society International, Inc., 140 S. Ct. 2082 (2020). In an opinion by Justice Kavanaugh, the Court held that outcome was driven by "two bedrock principles of American constitutional law and American corporate law . . . ." First, "that foreign citizens outside U.S. territory do not possess rights under the U.S. Constitution" and second, "that separately incorporated organizations are separate legal units with distinct legal rights and obligations." These together, Justice Kavanaugh wrote, "lead to a simple conclusion: As foreign organizations operating abroad, plaintiffs' foreign affiliates possess no rights under the First Amendment." Justice Breyer, along with Justices Ginsburg and Sotomayor, dissented; Justice Breyer argued that "clearly identified affiliates that have been incorporated overseas" should enjoy the same First Amendment rights as the American organizations with whom they are affiliated. Justice Kagan did not participate.

Page 1046: Insert the following paragraph before note 4:

Shurtleff v. Boston, ___ S. Ct. ___ (2022). Boston allowed private groups to fly flags of various types from one of flagpoles in front of City Hall. When a group called Camp Constitution requested permission to fly a Christian flag, the City refused — something it had not done previously. The director of the group sued, claiming that the City had engaged in viewpoint discrimination. The City argued that it was engaged in government speech. The majority thought the facts of the case were closer to *Matal* than to *Pleasant Grove.* From all evidence, the City never considered the flags to represent government speech. "When a government does not speak for itself, it may not exclude speech based on 'religious viewpoint'; doing so 'constitutes impermissible viewpoint discrimination.'" Justices

Alito, Thomas, and Gorsuch concurred, but took exception to Justice Breyer's multi-factor approach to ascertaining whether the government was speaking for itself or not. For Justice Alito, a more rule-like approach was preferable, "government speech occurs if—but only if—a government purposefully expresses a message of its own through persons authorized to speak on its behalf, and in doing so, does not rely on a means that abridges private speech."

F.   *Expression Rights Implicit in the Free Speech Guarantee*

2.   Freedom of Association

Page 1075, insert after note 6:

AMERICANS FOR PROSPERITY FOUNDATION v. BONTA
Supreme Court of the United States.
141 S. Ct. 2373 (2021)

Chief Justice Roberts delivered the opinion of the Court, except as to Part II–B–1.

To solicit contributions in California, charitable organizations must disclose to the state Attorney General's Office the identities of their major donors. The State contends that having this information on hand makes it easier to police misconduct by charities. We must decide whether California's disclosure requirement violates the First Amendment right to free association.

I. The California Attorney General's Office is responsible for statewide law enforcement, including the supervision and regulation of charitable fundraising. Under state law, the Attorney General is authorized to "establish and maintain a register" of charitable organizations and to obtain "whatever information, copies of instruments, reports, and records are needed for the establishment and maintenance of the register." In order to operate and raise funds in California, charities generally must register with the Attorney General and renew their registrations annually. Over 100,000 charities are currently registered in the State, and roughly 60,000 renew their registrations each year.

California law empowers the Attorney General to make rules and regulations regarding the registration and renewal process. Pursuant to this regulatory authority, the Attorney General requires charities renewing their registrations to file copies of their Internal Revenue Service Form 990 [which] contains information regarding tax-exempt organizations' mission, leadership, and finances. Schedule B to Form 990—the document that gives rise to the present dispute—requires organizations to disclose the names and addresses of donors who have contributed more than $5,000 in a particular tax year (or, in some cases, who have given more than 2 percent of an organization's total contributions).

. . . Americans for Prosperity Foundation is a public charity that is "devoted to education and training about the principles of a free and open society, including free markets, civil liberties, immigration reform, and constitutionally limited government." Thomas More Law Center is a public interest law firm whose "mission is to protect religious freedom, free speech, family values, and the sanctity of human life." Since 2001, each petitioner has renewed its registration and has filed a copy of its Form 990 with the Attorney General [but out] of concern for their donors' anonymity . . . the petitioners have declined to file their Schedule Bs (or have filed only redacted versions) with the State.

For many years, the petitioners' reluctance to turn over donor information presented no problem because the Attorney General was not particularly zealous about collecting Schedule Bs. That changed in 2010, when the California Department of Justice "ramped up its efforts to enforce charities' Schedule B obligations, sending thousands of deficiency letters to charities that had not complied with the Schedule B requirement," [and threatened to deny them continued operation in the state.]

The petitioners each responded by filing suit in the Central District of California. In their complaints, they alleged that the Attorney General had violated their First Amendment rights and the rights of their donors. The petitioners alleged that disclosure of their Schedule Bs would make their donors less likely to contribute and would subject them to the risk of reprisals. Both organizations challenged the disclosure requirement on its face and as applied to them.

[The parties won a preliminary injunction in the district court, which was vacated by the Ninth Circuit. On remand, the parties again won, this time a permanent injunction; the district court found that the disclosure requirement because it was not narrowly tailored to the state's interest in preventing and investigating charitable misconduct. "The court credited testimony from California officials that Schedule Bs were rarely used to audit or investigate charities. And it found that even where Schedule B information was used, that information could be obtained from other sources." The district court "also determined that the disclosure regime burdened the associational rights of donors. In both cases, the court found that the petitioners had suffered from threats and harassment in the past, and that donors were likely to face similar retaliation in the future if their affiliations became publicly known."]

The District Court also found that California was unable to ensure the confidentiality of donors' information. During the course of litigation, the Foundation identified nearly 2,000 confidential Schedule Bs that had been inadvertently posted to the Attorney General's website, including dozens that were found the day before trial. . . . The court found after trial that "the amount of careless mistakes made by the Attorney General's Registry is shocking." And although California subsequently codified a policy prohibiting disclosure, the court determined that "[d]onors and potential donors would be reasonably justified in a fear of disclosure given such a context" of past breaches.

The Ninth Circuit again vacated the District Court's injunctions, and this time reversed the judgments and remanded for entry of judgment in favor of the Attorney General. The court held that the District Court had erred by imposing a narrow tailoring requirement. And it reasoned that the disclosure regime satisfied exacting scrutiny because the up-front collection of charities' Schedule Bs promoted investigative efficiency and effectiveness. The panel also found that the disclosure of Schedule Bs would not meaningfully burden donors' associational rights, in part because the Attorney General had taken remedial security measures to fix the confidentiality breaches identified at trial.

[The Ninth Circuit declined to rehear the case en banc and the Supreme Court granted certiorari.]

II.A. . . . This Court has "long understood as implicit in the right to engage in activities protected by the First Amendment a corresponding right to associate with others." . . . Government infringement of this freedom "can take a number of forms." We have held, for example, that the freedom of association may be violated where a group is required to take in members it does not want, where individuals are punished for their political affiliation, or where members of an organization are denied benefits based on the organization's message.

We have also noted that "[i]t is hardly a novel perception that compelled disclosure of affiliation with groups engaged in advocacy may constitute as effective a restraint on freedom of association as [other] forms of governmental action." *NAACP* v. *Alabama* involved this chilling effect in its starkest form. The NAACP opened an Alabama office that supported racial integration in higher education and public transportation. In response, NAACP members were threatened with economic reprisals and violence. As part of an effort to oust the organization from the State, the Alabama Attorney General sought the group's membership lists. We held that the First Amendment prohibited such compelled disclosure. [W]e noted "the vital relationship between freedom to associate and privacy in one's associations," Because NAACP members faced a risk of reprisals if their affiliation with the organization became known—and because Alabama had demonstrated no offsetting interest "sufficient to justify the deterrent effect" of disclosure—we concluded that the State's demand violated the First Amendment.

B. 1. *NAACP* v. *Alabama* did not phrase in precise terms the standard of review that applies to First Amendment challenges to compelled disclosure. We have since settled on a standard referred to as "exacting scrutiny." Under that standard, there must be "a substantial relation between the disclosure requirement and a sufficiently important governmental interest." "To withstand this scrutiny, the strength of the governmental interest must reflect the seriousness of the actual burden on First Amendment rights:" . . .

The Law Center (but not the Foundation) argues that we should apply strict scrutiny, not exacting scrutiny. . . . The Law Center contends that only strict scrutiny adequately protects the associational rights of charities. [T]he Law Center [argues] that [the Court's application of] exacting scrutiny [has been confined to cases arising in] the electoral context, where the government's important interests justify less searching review.

It is true that we first enunciated the exacting scrutiny standard in a campaign finance case. And we have since invoked it in other election-related settings. But exacting scrutiny is not unique to electoral disclosure regimes. To the contrary, [the test used in prior election cases] derived the test from *NAACP* v. *Alabama* itself, as well as other nonelection cases . . . Regardless of the type of association, compelled disclosure requirements are reviewed under exacting scrutiny.

2. The Law Center (now joined by the Foundation) argues in the alternative that even if exacting scrutiny applies, such review incorporates a least restrictive means test similar to the one imposed by strict scrutiny. The United States and the Attorney General respond that exacting scrutiny demands no additional tailoring beyond the "substantial relation" requirement noted above. We think that the answer lies between those two positions. While exacting scrutiny does not require that disclosure regimes be the least restrictive means of achieving their ends, it does require that they be narrowly tailored to the government's asserted interest.

The need for narrow tailoring was set forth early in our compelled disclosure cases. In *Shelton* v. *Tucker*, we considered an Arkansas statute that required teachers to disclose every organization to which they belonged or contributed. We acknowledged the importance of "the right of a State to investigate the competence and fitness of those whom it hires to teach in its schools" . . . But we nevertheless held that the Arkansas statute was invalid because even a "legitimate and substantial" governmental interest "cannot be pursued by means that broadly stifle fundamental personal liberties when the end can be more narrowly achieved."

. . . Narrow tailoring is crucial where First Amendment activity is chilled — even if indirectly — "[b]ecause First Amendment freedoms need breathing space to survive." . . .

. . . A substantial relation is necessary but not sufficient to ensure that the government adequately considers the potential for First Amendment harms before requiring that organizations reveal sensitive information about their members and supporters. Where exacting scrutiny applies, the challenged requirement must be narrowly tailored to the interest it promotes, even if it is not the least restrictive means of achieving that end.

The dissent [argues] that narrow tailoring is required only for disclosure regimes that "impose a severe burden on associational rights." Because, in the dissent's view, the petitioners have not shown such a burden here, narrow tailoring is not required.

We respectfully disagree. . . . Contrary to the dissent, we understand this Court's discussion of rules that are "broad" and "broadly stifle" First Amendment freedoms to refer to the scope of challenged restrictions — their breadth — rather than the severity of any demonstrated burden. . . .

... [A] reasonable assessment of the burdens imposed by disclosure should begin with an understanding of the extent to which the burdens are unnecessary, and that requires narrow tailoring. ...

* * *

The District Court correctly entered judgment in favor of the petitioners and permanently enjoined the Attorney General from collecting their Schedule Bs. The Ninth Circuit erred by vacating those injunctions and directing entry of judgment for the Attorney General. The judgment of the Ninth Circuit is reversed, and the cases are remanded for further proceedings consistent with this opinion. ...

JUSTICE THOMAS, concurring in Parts I, II–A, II–B–2, and III–A, and concurring in the judgment.

... [T]he bulk of "our precedents ... require application of strict scrutiny to laws that compel disclosure of protected First Amendment association." California's law fits that description. Although the Court rightly holds that even the less demanding "exacting scrutiny" standard requires narrow tailoring for laws that compel disclosure, invoking exacting scrutiny is at odds with our repeated recognition "that privacy of association is protected under the First Amendment." ... Laws directly burdening the right to associate anonymously, including compelled disclosure laws, should be subject to the same scrutiny as laws directly burdening other First Amendment rights. ...

JUSTICE ALITO, with whom JUSTICE GORSUCH joins, concurring in Parts I, II–A, II–B–2, and III, and concurring in the judgment.

I am pleased to join most of The Chief Justice's opinion. In particular, I agree that the exacting scrutiny standard drawn from our election-law jurisprudence has real teeth. It requires both narrow tailoring and consideration of alternative means of obtaining the sought-after information. For the reasons The Chief Justice explains, California's blunderbuss approach to charitable disclosures fails exacting scrutiny and is facially unconstitutional. The question is not even close. And for the same reasons, California's approach necessarily fails strict scrutiny. ...

[However, because] the choice between exacting and strict scrutiny has no effect on the decision in these cases, I see no need to decide which standard should be applied here or whether the same level of scrutiny should apply in all cases in which the compelled disclosure of associations is challenged under the First Amendment.

JUSTICE SOTOMAYOR, with whom JUSTICE BREYER and JUSTICE KAGAN join, dissenting.

Although this Court is protective of First Amendment rights, it typically requires that plaintiffs demonstrate an actual First Amendment burden before demanding that a law be narrowly tailored to the government's interests, never mind striking the law down in its entirety. Not so today. Today, the Court holds that reporting and disclosure requirements must be narrowly tailored even if a plaintiff demonstrates no burden at all. The same scrutiny the Court applied when NAACP members in the Jim Crow South did not want to disclose their membership for fear of reprisals and violence now applies equally in the case of donors only too happy to publicize their names across the websites and walls of the organizations they support.

California oversees nearly a quarter of this Nation's charitable assets. As part of that oversight, it investigates and prosecutes charitable fraud, relying in part on a registry where it collects and keeps charitable organizations' tax forms. The majority holds that a California regulation requiring charitable organizations to disclose tax forms containing the names and contributions of their top donors unconstitutionally burdens the right to associate even if the forms are not publicly disclosed.

In so holding, the Court discards its decades-long requirement that, to establish a cognizable burden on their associational rights, plaintiffs must plead and prove that disclosure will likely expose them to objective harms, such as threats, harassment, or reprisals. It also departs from the traditional, nuanced approach to First Amendment challenges, whereby the degree of means-end tailoring required is commensurate to the actual burdens on associational rights. Finally, it recklessly holds a state regulation facially invalid despite petitioners' failure to show that a substantial proportion of those affected would prefer anonymity, much less that they are objectively burdened by the loss of it.

Today's analysis marks reporting and disclosure requirements with a bull's-eye. Regulated entities who wish to avoid their obligations can do so by vaguely waving toward First Amendment "privacy concerns." It does not matter if not a single individual risks experiencing a single reprisal from disclosure, or if the vast majority of those affected would happily comply. That is all irrelevant to the Court's determination that California's Schedule B requirement is facially unconstitutional. Neither precedent nor common sense supports such a result. I respectfully dissent. . . .

NOTES

1. A New Standard of Review? What is the difference, precisely, between "exacting scrutiny" and intermediate scrutiny? Between it and strict scrutiny? Is it simply a relaxation of the means-ends fit? Or does the majority suggest that the government has a lesser burden when it comes to offering reasons for regulating in the first place?

2. Requiem for Disclosure Laws? Justice Sotomayor warns that the decision places a "bull's-eye" on laws that, for example, require candidates to disclose names of their donors. Do you think her fears are well-founded? Or might the reasons government have for requiring disclosure—namely, avoiding corruption or the appearance of corruption—be sufficient to justify disclosure so other voters can see who is financially supporting a candidate?

3. Is Form 990 Constitutional? Note that Schedule B is required to be filed with Form 990 under the IRS's regulations. Is the constitutionality of Form 990 now in doubt as a result of this decision? Do the state and federal governments have different interests in requiring disclosure? If so, would those differences have constitutional significance?

G.   *Free Expression and the Political Process*

1.   **Money as Speech: Political Contributions and Expenditures**

Page 1121: Insert the following note after note 3:

4. *Cruz for Senate:* **Candidate Reimbursement Limits.** *Federal Election Commission v. Cruz for Senate, 142 S. Ct. 1638 (2022).* The Court continued to chip away at BCRA's provisions by holding that provisions limiting the amount that candidates may accept after election to repay campaign debts violated the First Amendment. Senator Ted Cruz loaned his campaign committee $260,000 to set up a challenge to the provision of BCRA limiting the amount the campaign may use to repay loans to $250,000. "By restricting the sources of funds that campaigns may use to repay candidate loans," Chief Justice Roberts wrote, the limit "increases the risk that such loans will not be repaid. That in turn inhibits candidates from loaning money to their campaigns in the first place, burdening core speech." He further noted that the limit put challengers at a disadvantage relative to incumbents because "personal loans will sometimes be the only way for an unknown challenger with limited connections to frontload campaign spending." It rejected the government's argument that limits on loan repayment by the campaign was necessary to prevent actual and apparent corruption. It argued that because such donations come after the candidate is successful, at least the appearance that the donor would enjoy access was inevitable. But Chief Justice Roberts observed that "the government is unable to identify a single case of *quid pro quo* corruption in this context—even though most States do not impose a limit on the use of post-election contributions to repay candidate loans." Justice Kagan dissented for herself and Justices Breyer and Sotomayor.

Chapter 10

The Religion Clauses

B. The Free Exercise Clause

2. Legislation That Targets Religious Conduct or Belief

Page 1173: Insert new note 4:

4. Tandon v. Newton. California restricted private gatherings, including religious services, to gatherings no more than three households as part of its COVID mitigation strategy. However, it permitted other, secular indoor activities to continue with fewer restrictions. In a per curiam opinion, the Supreme Court invalidated those restrictions. Tandon v. Newton, 141 S. Ct. 1294 (2021) (per curiam). According to the Court, its cases stand for the following principles. First, "government regulations are not neutral and generally applicable, and therefore trigger strict scrutiny under the Free Exercise Clause, whenever they treat *any* comparable secular activity more favorably than religious exercise." Second, "whether two activities are comparable . . . must be judged against the asserted governmental interest that justifies the regulation at issue." In other words, if COVID spread is the concern, the state must prove that it is more likely to spread at an indoor worship service than at a gym, hair salon, restaurant, etc. Third, "the government has the burden to establish the challenged law satisfies strict scrutiny." Finally, withdrawal of a restriction does not moot a case where applicants "remain under a constant threat" that officials will reimpose restrictions. Justices Kagan, Breyer, and Sotomayor dissented.

Page 1174: Insert after renumbered note 5:

FULTON v. PHILADELPHIA
Supreme Court of the United States
141 S. Ct. 1868 (2021)

CHIEF JUSTICE ROBERTS delivered the opinion of the Court.

Catholic Social Services is a foster care agency in Philadelphia. The City stopped referring children to CSS upon discovering that the agency would not certify same-sex couples to be foster parents due to its religious beliefs about marriage. The City will renew its foster care contract with CSS only if the agency agrees to certify same-sex couples. The question presented is whether the actions of Philadelphia violate the First Amendment.

I. The Catholic Church has served the needy children of Philadelphia for over two centuries. In 1798, a priest in the City organized an association to care for orphans whose parents had died in a yellow fever epidemic. During the 19th century, nuns ran asylums for orphaned and destitute youth. When criticism of asylums mounted in the Progressive Era, the Church established the Catholic Children's Bureau to place children in foster homes. Petitioner CSS continues that mission today.

The Philadelphia foster care system depends on cooperation between the City and private foster agencies like CSS. When children cannot remain in their homes, the City's Department of Human Services assumes custody of them. The Department enters standard annual contracts with private foster agencies to place some of those children with foster families.

The placement process begins with review of prospective foster families. Pennsylvania law gives the authority to certify foster families to state-licensed foster agencies like CSS. Before certifying a family, an agency must conduct a home study during which it considers statutory criteria including the family's "ability to provide care, nurturing and supervision to children," "[e]xisting family relationships," and ability "to work in partnership" with a foster agency. The agency must decide whether to "approve, disapprove or provisionally approve the foster family."

When the Department seeks to place a child with a foster family, it sends its contracted agencies a request, known as a referral. The agencies report whether any of their certified families are available, and the Department places the child with what it regards as the most suitable family. The agency continues to support the family throughout the placement.

The religious views of CSS inform its work in this system. CSS believes that "marriage is a sacred bond between a man and a woman." Because the agency understands the certification of prospective foster families to be an endorsement of their relationships, it will not certify unmarried couples — regardless of their sexual orientation — or same-sex married couples. CSS does not object to certifying gay or lesbian individuals as single foster parents or to placing gay and lesbian children. No same-sex couple has ever sought certification from CSS. If one did, CSS would direct the couple to one of the more than 20 other agencies in the City, all of which currently certify same-sex couples. For over 50 years, CSS successfully contracted with the City to provide foster care services while holding to these beliefs.

But things changed in 2018. After receiving a complaint about a different agency, a newspaper ran a story in which a spokesman for the Archdiocese of Philadelphia stated that CSS would not be able to consider prospective foster parents in same-sex marriages. The City Council called for an investigation, saying that the City had "laws in place to protect its people from discrimination that occurs under the guise of religious freedom." The Philadelphia Commission on Human Relations launched an inquiry. And the Commissioner of the Department of Human Services held a meeting with the leadership of CSS. . . . Immediately after the meeting, the Department informed CSS that it would no longer refer children to the agency. The City later explained that the refusal of CSS to certify same-sex couples violated a non-discrimination provision in its contract with the City as well as the non-discrimination requirements of the citywide Fair Practices Ordinance. The City stated that it would not enter a full foster care contract with CSS in the future unless the agency agreed to certify same-sex couples.

CSS and three foster parents affiliated with the agency filed suit against the City, the Department, and the Commission. . . . CSS alleged that the referral freeze violated the Free Exercise and Free Speech Clauses of the First Amendment. . . .

[The district court denied CSS's request for a preliminary injunction, concluding that "that the contractual non-discrimination requirement and the Fair Practices Ordinance were neutral and generally applicable under *Employment Division, Department of Human Resources of Oregon v. Smith*, and that the free exercise claim was therefore unlikely to succeed." The Third Circuit affirmed the district court.]

CSS and the foster parents sought review. They challenged the Third Circuit's determination that the City's actions were permissible under *Smith* and also asked this Court to reconsider that precedent. . . .

We granted certiorari.

II. A. . . . As an initial matter, it is plain that the City's actions have burdened CSS's religious exercise by putting it to the choice of curtailing its mission or approving relationships inconsistent with its beliefs. The City disagrees. In its view, certification reflects only that foster parents satisfy the statutory criteria, not that the agency endorses their relationships. But CSS believes that certification is tantamount to endorsement. And "religious beliefs need not be acceptable, logical, consistent, or comprehensible to others in order to merit First Amendment protection." Our task is to decide whether the burden the City has placed on the religious exercise of CSS is constitutionally permissible.

Smith held that laws incidentally burdening religion are ordinarily not subject to strict scrutiny under the Free Exercise Clause so long as they are neutral and generally applicable. CSS urges us to overrule *Smith*, and the concurrences in the judgment argue in favor of doing so. But we need not revisit that decision here. This case falls outside *Smith* because the City has burdened the religious exercise of CSS through policies that do not meet the requirement of being neutral and generally applicable.

Government fails to act neutrally when it proceeds in a manner intolerant of religious beliefs or restricts practices because of their religious nature. CSS points to evidence in the record that it believes demonstrates that the City has transgressed this neutrality standard, but we find it more straightforward to resolve this case under the rubric of general applicability.

A law is not generally applicable if it "invite[s]" the government to consider the particular reasons for a person's conduct by providing "'a mechanism for individualized exemptions.'" For example, in *Sherbert v. Verner*, a Seventh-day Adventist was fired because she would not work on Saturdays. Unable to find a job that would allow her to keep the Sabbath as her faith required, she applied for unemployment benefits. The State denied her application under a law prohibiting eligibility to claimants who had "failed, without good cause . . . to accept available suitable work." We held that the denial infringed her free exercise rights and could be justified only by a compelling interest.

Smith later explained that the unemployment benefits law in *Sherbert* was not generally applicable because the "good cause" standard permitted the government to grant exemptions based on the circumstances underlying each application. *Smith* went on to hold that "where the State has in place a system of individual exemptions, it may not refuse to extend that system to cases of 'religious hardship' without compelling reason."

A law also lacks general applicability if it prohibits religious conduct while permitting secular conduct that undermines the government's asserted interests in a similar way. In *Church of Lukumi Babalu Aye, Inc. v. Hialeah*, for instance, the City of Hialeah adopted several ordinances prohibiting animal sacrifice, a practice of the Santeria faith. The City claimed that the ordinances were necessary in part to protect public health, which was "threatened by the disposal of animal carcasses in open public places." But the ordinances did not regulate hunters' disposal of their kills or improper garbage disposal by restaurants, both of which posed a similar hazard. The Court concluded that this and other forms of underinclusiveness meant that the ordinances were not generally applicable.

B. The City initially argued that CSS's practice violated section 3.21 of its standard foster care contract. We conclude, however, that this provision is not generally applicable as required by *Smith*. The current version of section 3.21 specifies in pertinent part:

> "**Rejection of Referral**. Provider shall not reject a child or family including, but not limited to, . . . prospective foster or adoptive parents, for Services based upon . . . their . . . sexual orientation . . . unless an exception is granted by the Commissioner or the Commissioner's designee, in his/her sole discretion."

This provision requires an agency to provide "Services," defined as "the work to be performed under this Contract," App. 560, to prospective foster parents regardless of their sexual orientation.

Like the good cause provision in *Sherbert*, section 3.21 incorporates a system of individual exemptions, made available in this case at the "sole discretion" of the Commissioner. The City has made clear that the Commissioner "has no intention of granting an exception" to CSS. But the City "may not refuse to extend that [exemption] system to cases of 'religious hardship' without compelling reason."

The City and intervenor-respondents resist this conclusion on several grounds. They first argue that governments should enjoy greater leeway under the Free Exercise Clause when setting rules for contractors than when regulating the general public. The government, they observe, commands heightened powers when managing its internal operations. And when individuals enter into government employment or contracts, they accept certain restrictions on their freedom as part of the deal. Given this context, the City and intervenor-respondents contend, the government should have a freer hand when dealing with contractors like CSS.

These considerations cannot save the City here. As Philadelphia rightly acknowledges, "principles of neutrality and general applicability still constrain the government in its capacity as manager." We have never suggested that the government may discriminate against religion when acting in its managerial role. And *Smith* itself drew support for the neutral and generally applicable standard from cases involving internal government affairs. The City and intervenor-respondents accordingly ask only that courts apply a more deferential approach in determining whether a policy is neutral and generally applicable in the contracting context. . . . No matter the level of deference we extend to the City, the inclusion of a formal system of entirely discretionary exceptions in section 3.21 renders the contractual non-discrimination requirement not generally applicable.

Perhaps all this explains why the City now contends that section 3.21 does not apply to CSS's refusal to certify same-sex couples after all. Instead, the City says that section 3.21 addresses only "an agency's right to refuse 'referrals' to place a child with a certified foster family." We think the City had it right the first time. Although the section is titled "Rejection of Referral," the text sweeps more broadly, forbidding the rejection of "prospective foster . . . parents" for "Services," without limitation. . . . Moreover, the City adopted the current version of section 3.21 shortly after declaring that it would make CSS's obligation to certify same-sex couples "explicit" in future contracts, confirming our understanding of the text of the provision.

The City and intervenor-respondents add that, notwithstanding the system of exceptions in section 3.21, a separate provision in the contract independently prohibits discrimination in the certification of foster parents. That provision, section 15.1, bars discrimination on the basis of sexual orientation, and it does not on its face allow for exceptions. But state law makes clear that "one part of a contract cannot be so interpreted as to annul another part." [A]n exception from section 3.21 also must govern the prohibition in section 15.1, lest the City's reservation of the authority to grant such an exception be a nullity. . . .

Finally, the City and intervenor-respondents contend that the availability of exceptions under section 3.21 is irrelevant because the Commissioner has never granted one. That misapprehends the issue. The creation of a formal mechanism for granting exceptions renders a policy not generally applicable, regardless whether any exceptions have been given, because it "invite[s]" the government to decide which reasons for not complying with the policy are worthy of solicitude — here, at the Commissioner's "sole discretion." . . .

C. In addition to relying on the contract, the City argues that CSS's refusal to certify same-sex couples constitutes an "Unlawful Public Accommodations Practice[]" in violation of the Fair Practices Ordinance. That ordinance forbids "deny[ing] or interfer[ing] with the public accommodations opportunities of an individual or otherwise discriminat[ing] based on his or her race, ethnicity, color, sex, sexual orientation, . . . disability, marital status, familial status," or several other protected categories. The City contends that foster care agencies are public accommodations and therefore forbidden from discriminating on the basis of sexual orientation when certifying foster parents.

CSS counters that "foster care has never been treated as a 'public accommodation' in Philadelphia." In any event, CSS adds, the ordinance cannot qualify as generally applicable because the City allows exceptions to it for secular reasons despite denying one for CSS's religious exercise. But that constitutional issue arises only if the ordinance applies to CSS in the first place. We conclude that it does not because foster care agencies do not act as public accommodations in performing certifications.

The ordinance defines a public accommodation in relevant part as "[a]ny place, provider or public conveyance, whether licensed or not, which solicits or accepts the patronage or trade of the public or whose goods, services, facilities, privileges, advantages or accommodations are extended, offered, sold, or otherwise made available to the public." Certification is not "made available to the public" in the usual sense of the words. . . . Related state law illustrates the same point. . . . The "common theme" is that a public accommodation must "provide a benefit to the general public allowing individual members of the general public to avail themselves of that benefit if they so desire."

Certification as a foster parent . . . is not readily accessible to the public. It involves a customized and selective assessment that bears little resemblance to staying in a hotel, eating at a restaurant, or riding a bus. . . .

III. . . . A government policy can survive strict scrutiny only if it advances "interests of the highest order" and is narrowly tailored to achieve those interests. Put another way, so long as the government can achieve its interests in a manner that does not burden religion, it must do so.

The City asserts that its non-discrimination policies serve three compelling interests: maximizing the number of foster parents, protecting the City from liability, and ensuring equal treatment of prospective foster parents and foster children. The City states these objectives at a high level of generality, but the First Amendment demands a more precise analysis. Rather than rely on "broadly formulated interests," courts must "scrutinize[] the asserted harm of granting specific exemptions to particular religious claimants." The question, then, is not whether the City has a compelling interest in enforcing its non-discrimination policies generally, but whether it has such an interest in denying an exception to CSS.

Once properly narrowed, the City's asserted interests are insufficient. Maximizing the number of foster families and minimizing liability are important goals, but the City fails to show that granting CSS an exception will put those goals at risk. If anything, including CSS in the program seems likely to increase, not reduce, the number of available foster parents. As for liability, the City offers only speculation that it might be sued over CSS's certification practices. Such speculation is insufficient to satisfy strict scrutiny, particularly because the authority to certify foster families is delegated to agencies by the State, not the City.

That leaves the interest of the City in the equal treatment of prospective foster parents and foster children. We do not doubt that this interest is a weighty one, for "[o]ur society has come to the recognition that gay persons and gay couples cannot be treated as social outcasts or as inferior in dignity and worth." On the facts of this case, however, this interest cannot justify denying CSS an exception for its religious exercise. The creation of a system of exceptions under the contract undermines the City's contention that its non-discrimination policies can brook no departures. The City offers no compelling reason why it has a particular interest in denying an exception to CSS while making them available to others.

* * *

. . . CSS seeks only an accommodation that will allow it to continue serving the children of Philadelphia in a manner consistent with its religious beliefs; it does not seek to impose those beliefs on anyone else. The refusal of Philadelphia to contract with CSS for the provision of foster care services unless it agrees to certify same-sex couples as foster parents cannot survive strict scrutiny, and violates the First Amendment.

In view of our conclusion that the actions of the City violate the Free Exercise Clause, we need not consider whether they also violate the Free Speech Clause.

The judgment of the United States Court of Appeals for the Third Circuit is reversed, and the case is remanded for further proceedings consistent with this opinion. . . .

JUSTICE BARRETT, with whom JUSTICE KAVANAUGH joins, and with whom JUSTICE BREYER joins as to all but the first paragraph, concurring.

In *Employment Div., Dept. of Human Resources of Ore. v. Smith*, this Court held that a neutral and generally applicable law typically does not violate the Free Exercise Clause — no matter how severely that law burdens religious exercise. Petitioners, their *amici*, scholars, and Justices of this Court have made serious arguments that *Smith* ought to be overruled. While history looms large in this debate, I find the historical record more silent than supportive on the question whether the founding generation understood the First Amendment to require religious exemptions from generally applicable laws in at least some circumstances. In my view, the textual and structural arguments against *Smith* are more compelling. As a matter of text and structure, it is difficult to see why the Free

Exercise Clause—lone among the First Amendment freedoms—offers nothing more than protection from discrimination.

Yet what should replace *Smith*? The prevailing assumption seems to be that strict scrutiny would apply whenever a neutral and generally applicable law burdens religious exercise. But I am skeptical about swapping *Smith*'s categorical antidiscrimination approach for an equally categorical strict scrutiny regime, particularly when this Court's resolution of conflicts between generally applicable laws and other First Amendment rights—like speech and assembly—has been much more nuanced. There would be a number of issues to work through if *Smith* were overruled. To name a few: Should entities like Catholic Social Services—which is an arm of the Catholic Church—be treated differently than individuals? Should there be a distinction between indirect and direct burdens on religious exercise? What forms of scrutiny should apply? And if the answer is strict scrutiny, would pre-*Smith* cases rejecting free exercise challenges to garden-variety laws come out the same way?

We need not wrestle with these questions in this case, though, because the same standard applies regardless whether *Smith* stays or goes. . . . As the Court's opinion today explains, the government contract at issue provides for individualized exemptions from its nondiscrimination rule, thus triggering strict scrutiny. And all nine Justices agree that the City cannot satisfy strict scrutiny. I therefore see no reason to decide in this case whether *Smith* should be overruled, much less what should replace it. . . .

[Justice Alito, joined by Justices Thomas and Gorsuch, penned a lengthy concurrence making the case that

> We should reconsider *Smith* without further delay. The correct interpretation of the Free Exercise Clause is a question of great importance, and *Smith*'s interpretation is hard to defend. It can't be squared with the ordinary meaning of the text of the Free Exercise Clause or with the prevalent understanding of the scope of the free-exercise right at the time of the First Amendment's adoption. It swept aside decades of established precedent, and it has not aged well. Its interpretation has been undermined by subsequent scholarship on the original meaning of the Free Exercise Clause. Contrary to what many initially expected, *Smith* has not provided a clear-cut rule that is easy to apply, and experience has disproved the *Smith* majority's fear that retention of the Court's prior free-exercise jurisprudence would lead to "anarchy."]

[A concurring opinion by Justice Gorsuch is omitted.]

NOTES

1. A Hollow Victory? In his concurring opinion, Justice Alito wrote that

> This decision might as well be written on the dissolving paper sold in magic shops. The City has been adamant about pressuring CSS to give in, and if the City wants

to get around today's decision, it can simply eliminate the never-used exemption power. If it does that, then, voilà, today's decision will vanish — and the parties will be back where they started. The City will claim that it is protected by *Smith*; CSS will argue that *Smith* should be overruled; the lower courts, bound by *Smith*, will reject that argument; and CSS will file a new petition in this Court challenging *Smith*. What is the point of going around in this circle?

Doesn't he have a point? Isn't it quite likely that Philadelphia will just eliminate the never-granted exemption and *then* refuse referrals to CSS?

2. On the Other Hand . . . Justice Barrett raises an important question the Court would have to confront should it overrule *Smith* — what comes after? Are there easy answers to the questions she poses that the Court would, eventually, have to confront?

3. Antonin the Fainthearted. During his time on the Court, Justice Scalia was, along with Justice Thomas, an ardent proponent of originalism, in part as a way of curbing the discretion of judges and ensuring that what was being enforced was the supreme law of the land and not judges' policy preferences. He defended originalism as "the lesser evil" in an oft-cited article published in 1989. Scalia, Originalism: The Lesser Evil, 57 U. Cin. L. Rev. 849 (1989). Given his enthusiasm for originalism, is it surprising in retrospect that Justice Scalia made no inquiry into the original public understanding of the Free Exercise Clause in *Smith*, as Justice Alito did in his lengthy concurring opinion? One clue might be that in that same article, he supposed that "in a crunch I may prove a fainthearted originalist." Perhaps he felt the consequences of allowing objections to generally-applicable laws for the religiously scrupulous might be undesirable in a religiously plural country like the United States.

Page 1183: Insert after note 2:

3. Espinoza v. Montana Department of Revenue. Montana's legislature established a program granting tax credits to those who donated to organizations that granted scholarships for private school tuition. The Montana Supreme Court struck down the program citing a provision of the state constitution prohibiting aid to schools "controlled by a 'church, sect, or denomination.'" Relying on *Trinity Lutheran*, a majority of the Court held that the state constitutional provision violated the Free Exercise Clause. Espinzoa v. Montana Department of Revenue, 140 S. Ct. 2246 (2020). As in *Trinity Lutheran* "Montana's no-aid provision bars religious schools from public benefits solely because of the religious character of the schools." In his opinion, the Chief Justice declined to apply *Locke v. Davey*, finding two key differences between the cases. As in *Trinity Lutheran,* the "the no-aid provision bars all aid to a religious school 'simply because of what it is,' putting the school to a choice between being religious or receiving government benefits." In *Locke*, "Washington had 'merely chosen not to fund a distinct category of instruction': the 'essentially religious endeavor' of training a minister . . . ." Second, "*Locke* invoked a 'historic and substantial' state interest in not funding the training of clergy" that had no counterpart in the current case.

In its attempt to satisfy strict scrutiny, the state claimed that it had an interest in preventing tax payer money from being diverted to sectarian institutions and, in so doing, actually promoted religious freedom. It also claimed an interest in separating church and state more strictly than the Establishment Clause required. Finally, it claimed an interest in supporting public education by preventing the diversion of aid from public to private schools. The Chief Justice noted that the Free Exercise Clause operates as a limit on how much separation states can mandate. He was skeptical of the religious freedom argument as well: "[T]his Court has repeatedly upheld government programs that spend taxpayer funds on equal aid to religious observers and organizations, particularly when the link between government and religion is attenuated by private choices." While a school might hesitate to participate in a program for fear of governmental interference in its religious activities, "we doubt that the school's liberty is enhanced by eliminating any option to participate in the first place." A for the impact on public schools, he noted that argument is "fatally underinclusive because its 'proffered objectives are not pursued with respect to nonreligious conduct'" because private, secular schools are permitted to participate. He concluded, "[a] State need not subsidize private education. But once a State decides to do so, it cannot disqualify some private schools solely because they are religious."

Justice Thomas wrote a concurring opinion in which he argued that the Court's expansive reading of the Establishment Clause had caused it to adopt a cramped view of the Free Exercise Clause. Justice Alito concurred as well; he argued that Montana's no-aid provision and those like it in other state constitutions were adopted because of Anti-Catholic bias and are unconstitutional for that reason. Justice Gorsuch, too, concurred to dispute the constitutional significance of religious "status" versus religious "use"—the distinction the Court made between *Locke* and *Trinity Lutheran*—suggesting he might have found himself dissenting in *Locke*. In the main dissent, Justice Breyer—joined in part by Justice Kagan—worried that requiring the participation of sectarian institutions in public benefits program could sow division and conflict.

Private choice cannot help the taxpayer who does not want to finance the propagation of religious beliefs, whether his own or someone else's. It will not help religious minorities too few in number to support a school that teaches their beliefs. And it will not satisfy those whose religious beliefs preclude them from participating in a government-sponsored program. Some or many of the persons who fit these descriptions may well feel ignored—or worse—when public funds are channeled to religious schools. These feelings may, in turn, sow religiously inspired political conflict and division—a risk that is considerably greater where States are *required* to include religious schools in programs like the one before us here. And it is greater still where, as here, those programs benefit only a handful of a State's many religious denominations.

4. Carson v. Makin. Parents of students who live in school districts that do not have secondary schools may receive tuition vouchers from the state to defray the costs of sending their child to a public or private secondary school of their choice. In order to be eligible for the tuition reimbursement, however, private schools must be non-sectarian. In Carson v. Makin, 2022 WL 2203333, the Supreme Court concluded that the exclusion of private, religious schools violated the Free Exercise Clause. Reviewing the holdings in the earlier cases, Chief Justice Roberts concluded that:

> The "unremarkable" principles applied in *Trinity Lutheran* and *Espinoza* suffice to resolve this case. Maine offers its citizens a benefit: tuition assistance payments for any family whose school district does not provide a public secondary school. Just like the wide range of nonprofit organizations eligible to receive playground resurfacing grants in *Trinity Lutheran*, a wide range of private schools are eligible to receive Maine tuition assistance payments here. And like the daycare center in *Trinity Lutheran*, [sectarian private schools] are disqualified from this generally available benefit "solely because of their religious character." By "condition[ing] the availability of benefits" in that manner, Maine's tuition assistance program — like the program in *Trinity Lutheran* — "effectively penalizes the free exercise" of religion.

The Court rejected Maine's argument that it had a compelling interest in maintaining a separation of church and state. "A State's antiestablishment interest," the Chief Justice wrote, "does not justify enactments that exclude some members of the community from an otherwise generally available benefit because of their religious exercise." It also rejected the state's argument that because the purpose of the vouchers was to ensure all students would receive the equivalent of a public education, the institution delivering the education must be secular. It could have operated its own school, the Court noted, but chose the tuition reimbursement instead. Therefore, "Maine's administration of that benefit is subject to the free exercise principles governing any such public benefit program — including the prohibition on denying the benefit based on a recipient's religious exercise."

Justice Breyer criticized the majority for weakening the Establishment Clause and ignoring *Locke*'s "play in the joints" doctrine.

> The First Amendment begins by forbidding the government from "mak[ing] [any] law respecting an establishment of religion." It next forbids them to make any law "prohibiting the free exercise thereof." The Court today pays almost no attention to the words in the first Clause while giving almost exclusive attention to the words in the second. The majority also fails to recognize the " 'play in the joints' " between the two Clauses. That "play" gives States some degree of legislative leeway. It sometimes allows a State to further antiestablishment interests by withholding aid from religious institutions without violating the Constitution's protections for the free exercise of religion. In my view, Maine's nonsectarian requirement falls squarely within the scope of that constitutional leeway. I respectfully dissent.

Consider the status of the notion of *Locke v. Davey* and the "play in the joints" between the Free Exercise and Establishment Clauses as you read the next case.

KENNEDY v. BREMERTON SCHOOL DISTRICT
Supreme Court of the United States.
2022 WL 2295034

JUSTICE GORSUCH delivered the opinion of the Court.

Joseph Kennedy lost his job as a high school football coach because he knelt at midfield after games to offer a quiet prayer of thanks. Mr. Kennedy prayed during a period when school employees were free to speak with a friend, call for a reservation at a restaurant, check email, or attend to other personal matters. He offered his prayers quietly while his students were otherwise occupied. Still, the Bremerton School District disciplined him anyway. It did so because it thought anything less could lead a reasonable observer to conclude (mistakenly) that it endorsed Mr. Kennedy's religious beliefs. That reasoning was misguided. Both the Free Exercise and Free Speech Clauses of the First Amendment protect expressions like Mr. Kennedy's. Nor does a proper understanding of the Amendment's Establishment Clause require the government to single out private religious speech for special disfavor. The Constitution and the best of our traditions counsel mutual respect and tolerance, not censorship and suppression, for religious and nonreligious views alike.

I.A. [Kennedy had prayed midfield after games for seven years without anyone complaining. In addition, he would make pre-game motivational speeches that incorporated religious themes and continued the practice, which pre-dated him, of pregame or postgame prayer with players. Occasionally, players — both from his team and the opposing team — would join him for his post-game, midfield prayer. In September, 2015, the school district instructed Kennedy to avoid inspirational talks that alluded to religion and the supervision or encouragement of student prayer. His personal prayers, the letter continued, should be "nondemonstrative" in order to avoid the appearance of endorsement of religion by a public school employee. He briefly ceased his mid-field prayer, but resumed the practice in October, 2015. He informed the school district of this, but said that he would do this only after players and others had departed. Unwilling to pray privately, Kennedy continued to pray mid-field. In late October, he was put on administrative leave; and despite have received positive evaluations since his hiring, he received a poor evaluation in November, 2015 and did not return for thee next season. Kennedy sued in federal court, claiming the school district had violated his free speech and free exercise rights. The district court ruled against him, concluding that had the school district *not* disciplined him, it likely would have violated the Establishment Clause. The Ninth Circuit agreed and rejected a petition to rehear the case en banc, from which eleven judges dissented. The Supreme Court then granted certiorari.]

III. Now before us, Mr. Kennedy renews his argument that the District's conduct violated both the Free Exercise and Free Speech Clauses of the First Amendment. These Clauses work in tandem. Where the Free Exercise Clause protects religious exercises, whether communicative or not, the Free Speech Clause provides overlapping protection for expressive religious activities. That the First Amendment doubly protects religious speech is no accident. It is a natural outgrowth of the framers' distrust of government attempts to regulate religion and suppress dissent. . . .

A. The Free Exercise Clause provides that "Congress shall make no law . . . prohibiting the free exercise" of religion. This Court has held the Clause applicable to the States under the terms of the Fourteenth Amendment. The Clause protects not only the right to harbor religious beliefs inwardly and secretly. It does perhaps its most important work by protecting the ability of those who hold religious beliefs of all kinds to live out their faiths in daily life through "the performance of (or abstention from) physical acts."

Under this Court's precedents, a plaintiff may carry the burden of proving a free exercise violation in various ways, including by showing that a government entity has burdened his sincere religious practice pursuant to a policy that is not "neutral" or "generally applicable." Should a plaintiff make a showing like that, this Court will find a First Amendment violation unless the government can satisfy "strict scrutiny" by demonstrating its course was justified by a compelling state interest and was narrowly tailored in pursuit of that interest.

That Mr. Kennedy has discharged his burdens is effectively undisputed. No one questions that he seeks to engage in a sincerely motivated religious exercise. The exercise in question involves, as Mr. Kennedy has put it, giving "thanks through prayer" briefly and by himself "on the playing field" at the conclusion of each game he coaches. Mr. Kennedy has indicated repeatedly that he is willing to "wai[t] until the game is over and the players have left the field" to "wal[k] to mid-field to say [his] short, private, personal prayer." The contested exercise before us does not involve leading prayers with the team or before any other captive audience. Mr. Kennedy's "religious beliefs do not require [him] to lead any prayer . . . involving students." At the District's request, he voluntarily discontinued the school tradition of locker-room prayers and his postgame religious talks to students. The District disciplined him *only* for his decision to persist in praying quietly without his players after three games in October 2015.

Nor does anyone question that, in forbidding Mr. Kennedy's brief prayer, the District failed to act pursuant to a neutral and generally applicable rule. A government policy will not qualify as neutral if it is "specifically directed at . . . religious practice." A policy can fail this test if it "discriminate[s] on its face," or if a religious exercise is otherwise its "object." A government policy will fail the general applicability requirement if it "prohibits religious conduct while permitting secular conduct that undermines the government's asserted interests in a similar way," or if it provides "a mechanism for individualized exemptions."

Failing either the neutrality or general applicability test is sufficient to trigger strict scrutiny.

In this case, the District's challenged policies were neither neutral nor generally applicable. By its own admission, the District sought to restrict Mr. Kennedy's actions at least in part because of their religious character. As it put it in its September 17 letter, the District prohibited "any overt actions on Mr. Kennedy's part, appearing to a reasonable observer to endorse even voluntary, student-initiated prayer." The District further explained that it could not allow "an employee, while still on duty, to engage in *religious* conduct." Prohibiting a religious practice was thus the District's unquestioned "object." The District candidly acknowledged as much below, conceding that its policies were "not neutral" toward religion.

The District's challenged policies also fail the general applicability test. The District's performance evaluation after the 2015 football season advised against rehiring Mr. Kennedy on the ground that he "failed to supervise student-athletes after games." But, in fact, this was a bespoke requirement specifically addressed to Mr. Kennedy's religious exercise. The District permitted other members of the coaching staff to forgo supervising students briefly after the game to do things like visit with friends or take personal phone calls. Thus, any sort of postgame supervisory requirement was not applied in an evenhanded, across-the-board way. Again recognizing as much, the District conceded before the Ninth Circuit that its challenged directives were not "generally applicable."

[For the Court's treatment of Kennedy's free speech claim, see supra Chapter 9.D.3.]

IV. Whether one views the case through the lens of the Free Exercise or Free Speech Clause, at this point the burden shifts to the District. Under the Free Exercise Clause, a government entity normally must satisfy at least "strict scrutiny," showing that its restrictions on the plaintiff's protected rights serve a compelling interest and are narrowly tailored to that end. . . .

A. As we have seen, the District argues that its suspension of Mr. Kennedy was essential to avoid a violation of the Establishment Clause. On its account, Mr. Kennedy's prayers might have been protected by the Free Exercise and Free Speech Clauses. But his rights were in "direct tension" with the competing demands of the Establishment Clause. To resolve that clash, the District reasoned, Mr. Kennedy's rights had to "yield." . . .

But how could that be? It is true that this Court and others often refer to the "Establishment Clause," the "Free Exercise Clause," and the "Free Speech Clause" as separate units. But the three Clauses appear in the same sentence of the same Amendment . . . . A natural reading of that sentence would seem to suggest the Clauses have "complementary" purposes, not warring ones where one Clause is always sure to prevail over the others.

The District arrived at a different understanding this way. It began with the premise that the Establishment Clause is offended whenever a "reasonable observer" could conclude that the government has "endorse[d]" religion. The

District then took the view that a "reasonable observer" could think it "endorsed Kennedy's religious activity by not stopping the practice." On the District's account, it did not matter whether the Free Exercise Clause protected Mr. Kennedy's prayer. It did not matter if his expression was private speech protected by the Free Speech Clause. It did not matter that the District never actually endorsed Mr. Kennedy's prayer, no one complained that it had, and a strong public reaction only followed after the District sought to ban Mr. Kennedy's prayer. Because a reasonable observer could (mistakenly) infer that by allowing the prayer the District endorsed Mr. Kennedy's message, the District felt it had to act, even if that meant suppressing otherwise protected First Amendment activities. In this way, the District effectively created its own "vise between the Establishment Clause on one side and the Free Speech and Free Exercise Clauses on the other," placed itself in the middle, and then chose its preferred way out of its self-imposed trap.

To defend its approach, the District relied on *Lemon* and its progeny. . . .

An Establishment Clause violation does not automatically follow whenever a public school or other government entity "fail[s] to censor" private religious speech. Nor does the Clause "compel the government to purge from the public sphere" anything an objective observer could reasonably infer endorses or "partakes of the religious." In fact, just this Term the Court unanimously rejected a city's attempt to censor religious speech based on *Lemon* and the endorsement test.

In place of *Lemon* and the endorsement test, this Court has instructed that the Establishment Clause must be interpreted by " 'reference to historical practices and understandings.' " " '[T]he line' " that courts and governments "must draw between the permissible and the impermissible" has to " 'accor[d] with history and faithfully reflec[t] the understanding of the Founding Fathers.' " An analysis focused on original meaning and history, this Court has stressed, has long represented the rule rather than some " 'exception' " within the "Court's Establishment Clause jurisprudence." . . .

B. Perhaps sensing that the primary theory it pursued below rests on a mistaken understanding of the Establishment Clause, the District offers a backup argument in this Court. It still contends that its Establishment Clause concerns trump Mr. Kennedy's free exercise and free speech rights. But the District now seeks to supply different reasoning for that result. Now, it says, it was justified in suppressing Mr. Kennedy's religious activity because otherwise it would have been guilty of coercing students to pray. And, the District says, coercing worship amounts to an Establishment Clause violation on anyone's account of the Clause's original meaning. . . .

The evidence cannot sustain it. To be sure, this Court has long held that government may not, consistent with a historically sensitive understanding of the Establishment Clause, "make a religious observance compulsory." Government "may not coerce anyone to attend church," nor may it force citizens to engage in "a formal religious exercise." No doubt, too, coercion along these lines was among the foremost hallmarks of religious establishments the framers sought to prohibit when they adopted the First Amendment. Members of this Court have sometimes disagreed on what exactly qualifies as impermissible coercion in light of the original meaning of the Establishment Clause. But in this case Mr. Kennedy's private religious exercise did not come close to crossing any line one might imagine separating protected private expression from impermissible government coercion.

[T]he District conceded in a public 2015 document that there was "no evidence that students [were] directly coerced to pray with Kennedy." This is consistent with Mr. Kennedy's account too. He has repeatedly stated that he "never coerced, required, or asked any student to pray," and that he never "told any student that it was important that they participate in any religious activity.". . . .

The only prayer Mr. Kennedy sought to continue was the kind he had "started out doing" at the beginning of his tenure — the prayer he gave alone. He made clear that he could pray "while the kids were doing the fight song" and "take a knee by [him]self and give thanks and continue on." Mr. Kennedy even considered it "acceptable" to say his "prayer while the players were walking to the locker room" or "bus," and then catch up with his team. In short, Mr. Kennedy did not seek to direct any prayers to students or require anyone else to participate. His plan was to wait to pray until athletes were occupied, and he "told everybody" that's what he wished "to do." It was for three prayers of this sort alone in October 2015 that the District suspended him.

Naturally, Mr. Kennedy's proposal to pray quietly by himself on the field would have meant some people would have seen his religious exercise. Those close at hand might have heard him too. But learning how to tolerate speech or prayer of all kinds is "part of learning how to live in a pluralistic society," a trait of character essential to "a tolerant citizenry." This Court has long recognized as well that "secondary school students are mature enough . . . to understand that a school does not endorse," let alone coerce them to participate in, "speech that it merely permits on a nondiscriminatory basis." Of course, some will take offense to certain forms of speech or prayer they are sure to encounter in a society where those activities enjoy such robust constitutional protection. But "[o]ffense . . . does not equate to coercion."

The District responds that, as a coach, Mr. Kennedy "wielded enormous authority and influence over the students," and students might have felt compelled to pray alongside him. To support this argument, the District submits that, after Mr. Kennedy's suspension, a few parents told District employees that their sons had "participated in the team prayers only because they did not wish to separate themselves from the team."

This reply fails too. Not only does the District rely on hearsay to advance it. For all we can tell, the concerns the District says it heard from parents were occasioned by the locker-room prayers that predated Mr. Kennedy's tenure or his postgame religious talks, all of which he discontinued at the District's request.

There is no indication in the record that anyone expressed any coercion concerns to the District about the quiet, postgame prayers that Mr. Kennedy asked to continue and that led to his suspension. Nor is there any record evidence that students felt pressured to participate in these prayers. . . .

The absence of evidence of coercion in this record leaves the District to its final redoubt. Here, the District suggests that *any* visible religious conduct by a teacher or coach should be deemed—without more and as a matter of law—impermissibly coercive on students. In essence, the District asks us to adopt the view that the only acceptable government role models for students are those who eschew any visible religious expression. . . .

Such a rule would be a sure sign that our Establishment Clause jurisprudence had gone off the rails. In the name of protecting religious liberty, the District would have us suppress it. Rather than respect the First Amendment's double protection for religious expression, it would have us preference secular activity. Not only could schools fire teachers for praying quietly over their lunch, for wearing a yarmulke to school, or for offering a midday prayer during a break before practice. Under the District's rule, a school would be *required* to do so.

[T]his case looks very different from those in which this Court has found prayer involving public school students to be problematically coercive. . . . The prayers for which Mr. Kennedy was disciplined were not publicly broadcast or recited to a captive audience. Students were not required or expected to participate. And, in fact, none of Mr. Kennedy's students did participate in any of the three October 2015 prayers that resulted in Mr. Kennedy's discipline.

C. In the end, the District's case hinges on the need to generate conflict between an individual's rights under the Free Exercise and Free Speech Clauses and its own Establishment Clause duties—and then develop some explanation why one of these Clauses in the First Amendment should " 'trum[p]' " the other two. But the project falters badly. Not only does the District fail to offer a sound reason to prefer one constitutional guarantee over another. It cannot even show that they are at odds. In truth, there is no conflict between the constitutional commands before us. There is only the "mere shadow" of a conflict, a false choice premised on a misconstruction of the Establishment Clause. And in no world may a government entity's concerns about phantom constitutional violations justify actual violations of an individual's First Amendment rights.

V. Respect for religious expressions is indispensable to life in a free and diverse Republic—whether those expressions take place in a sanctuary or on a field, and whether they manifest through the spoken word or a bowed head. Here, a government entity sought to punish an individual for engaging in a brief, quiet, personal religious observance doubly protected by the Free Exercise and Free Speech Clauses of the First Amendment. And the only meaningful justification the government offered for its reprisal rested on a mistaken view that it had a duty to ferret out and suppress religious observances even as it allows comparable secular speech. The Constitution neither mandates nor tolerates that kind of discrimination. Mr. Kennedy is entitled to summary judgment on his First Amendment claims. The judgment of the Court of Appeals is

Reversed.

[Concurring opinions by Justices Thomas and Alito are omitted.]

JUSTICE SOTOMAYOR, with whom JUSTICE BREYER and JUSTICE KAGAN join, dissenting.

This case is about whether a public school must permit a school official to kneel, bow his head, and say a prayer at the center of a school event. The Constitution does not authorize, let alone require, public schools to embrace this conduct. Since *Engel v. Vitale*, this Court consistently has recognized that school officials leading prayer is constitutionally impermissible. Official-led prayer strikes at the core of our constitutional protections for the religious liberty of students and their parents, as embodied in both the Establishment Clause and the Free Exercise Clause of the First Amendment.

The Court now charts a different path, yet again paying almost exclusive attention to the Free Exercise Clause's protection for individual religious exercise while giving short shrift to the Establishment Clause's prohibition on state establishment of religion. To the degree the Court portrays petitioner Joseph Kennedy's prayers as private and quiet, it misconstrues the facts. The record reveals that Kennedy had a longstanding practice of conducting demonstrative prayers on the 50-yard line of the football field. Kennedy consistently invited others to join his prayers and for years led student athletes in prayer at the same time and location. The Court ignores this history. The Court also ignores the severe disruption to school events caused by Kennedy's conduct, viewing it as irrelevant because the Bremerton School District (District) stated that it was suspending Kennedy to avoid it being viewed as endorsing religion. Under the Court's analysis, presumably this would be a different case if the District had cited Kennedy's repeated disruptions of school programming and violations of school policy regarding public access to the field as grounds for suspending him. As the District did not articulate those grounds, the Court assesses only the District's Establishment Clause concerns. It errs by assessing them divorced from the context and history of Kennedy's prayer practice.

Today's decision goes beyond merely misreading the record. The Court over-rules *Lemon v. Kurtzman*, and calls into question decades of subsequent precedents that it deems "offshoot[s]" of that decision. In the process, the Court rejects longstanding concerns surrounding government endorsement of religion and replaces the standard for reviewing such questions with a new "history and tradition" test. In addition, while the Court reaffirms that the Establishment Clause prohibits the government from coercing participation in religious exercise, it applies a nearly toothless version of the coercion analysis, failing to acknowledge the unique pressures faced by students when participating in school-sponsored activities. This decision does a disservice to schools and the young citizens they serve, as well as to our Nation's longstanding commitment to the separation of church and state. I respectfully dissent.

II. Properly understood, this case is not about the limits on an individual's ability to engage in private prayer at work. This case is about whether a school district is required to allow one of its employees to incorporate a public, communicative display of the employee's personal religious beliefs into a school event, where that display is recognizable as part of a longstanding practice of the employee ministering religion to students as the public watched. A school district is not required to permit such conduct; in fact, the Establishment Clause prohibits it from doing so. . . .

A. Given the twin Establishment Clause concerns of endorsement and coercion, it is unsurprising that the Court has consistently held integrating prayer into public school activities to be unconstitutional, including when student participation is not a formal requirement or prayer is silent. The Court also has held that incorporating a nondenominational general benediction into a graduation ceremony is unconstitutional. Finally, this Court has held that including prayers in student football games is unconstitutional, even when delivered by students rather than staff and even when students themselves initiated the prayer. . . .

B. Kennedy's tradition of a 50-yard line prayer thus strikes at the heart of the Establishment Clause's concerns about endorsement. For students and community members at the game, Coach Kennedy was the face and the voice of the District during football games. The timing and location Kennedy selected for his prayers were "clothed in the traditional indicia of school sporting events." Kennedy spoke from the playing field, which was accessible only to students and school employees, not to the general public. Although the football game itself had ended, the football game events had not; Kennedy himself acknowledged that his responsibilities continued until the players went home. Kennedy's postgame responsibilities were what placed Kennedy on the 50-yard line in the first place; that was, after all, where he met the opposing team to shake hands after the game. Permitting a school coach to lead students and others he invited onto the field in prayer at a predictable time after each game could only be viewed as a postgame tradition occurring "with the approval of the school administration."

Kennedy's prayer practice also implicated the coercion concerns at the center of this Court's Establishment Clause jurisprudence. This Court has previously recognized a heightened potential for coercion where school officials are involved, as their "effort[s] to monitor prayer will be perceived by the students as inducing a participation they might otherwise reject." The reasons for fearing this pressure are self-evident. This Court has recognized that students face immense social pressure. Students look up to their teachers and coaches as role models and seek their approval. Students also depend on this approval for tangible benefits. Players recognize that gaining the coach's approval may pay dividends small and large, from extra playing time to a stronger letter of recommendation to additional support in college athletic recruiting. In addition to these pressures to please their coaches, this Court has recognized that players face "immense social pressure" from their peers in the "extracurricular event that is American high school football."

The record before the Court bears this out. The District Court found, in the evidentiary record, that some students reported joining Kennedy's prayer because they felt social pressure to follow their coach and teammates. Kennedy told the District that he began his prayers alone and that players followed each other over time until a majority of the team joined him, an evolution showing coercive pressure at work. . . .

Finally, Kennedy stresses that he never formally required students to join him in his prayers. But existing precedents do not require coercion to be explicit, particularly when children are involved. To the contrary, this Court's Establishment Clause jurisprudence establishes that " 'the government may no more use social pressure to enforce orthodoxy than it may use more direct means.' " Thus, the Court has held that the Establishment Clause "will not permit" a school " 'to exact religious conformity from a student as the price' of joining her classmates at a varsity football game." To uphold a coach's integration of prayer into the ceremony of a football game, in the context of an established history of the coach inviting student involvement in prayer, is to exact precisely this price from students. . . .

* * *

The Free Exercise Clause and Establishment Clause are equally integral in protecting religious freedom in our society. The first serves as "a promise from our government," while the second erects a "backstop that disables our government from breaking it" and "start[ing] us down the path to the past, when [the right to free exercise] was routinely abridged."

Today, the Court once again weakens the backstop. It elevates one individual's interest in personal religious exercise, in the exact time and place of that individual's choosing, over society's interest in protecting the separation between church and state, eroding the protections for religious liberty for all. Today's decision is particularly misguided because it elevates the religious rights of a school official, who voluntarily accepted public employment and the limits that public employment entails, over those of his students, who are required to attend school and who this Court has long recognized are particularly vulnerable and deserving of protection. In doing so, the Court sets us further down a perilous path in forcing States to entangle themselves with religion, with all of our rights hanging in the balance. As much as the Court protests otherwise, today's decision is no victory for religious liberty. I respectfully dissent.

NOTES

1. The End of "Play in the Joints?" Recall that in *Locke v. Davey*, the Court refused to hold that the state's refusal to subsidize Davey's pastoral studies did not violate the Free Exercise Clause, even if it *could have* done so without violating the Establishment Clause. Chief Justice Rehnquist said there needed to some "play in the joins" such that what the Establishment Clause didn't forbid, the Free Exercise didn't likewise *require*. Doesn't *Kennedy* suggest that doctrine no longer has much vitality?

2. Mistah Kurtz(man), He Dead? The dissent claims that the *Kennedy* majority overrules *Lemon v. Kurtzman*. Is that so?

3. Just the Facts. Notable is the differing characterization of Kennedy's actions in the majority and the dissent. Justice Gorsuch characterized Kennedy as engaging in a quiet, post-game prayer by himself when the players were occupied, headed to the locker room, or boarding the bus. Justice Sotomayor, on the other hand, called his actions severely disruptive and even included pictures showing players joining Kennedy in the field. (As has been pointed out, however, the players depicted included many players from opposing teams.) Does it matter to the analysis whose characterization is more accurate?

C. The Establishment Clause

5. Government Endorsement of Religious Belief or Nonbelief and Governmental Coercion to Believe or Not Believe

b. Other Government Adoption of Religious Symbols

Page 1238: Insert the following before section 3:

THE AMERICAN LEGION v. AMERICAN HUMANIST ASSOCIATION
Supreme Court of the United States
139 S.Ct. 2067 (2019)

JUSTICE ALITO announced the judgment of the Court and delivered the opinion of the Court with respect to Parts I, II–B, II–C, III, and IV, and an opinion with respect to Parts II–A and II–D, in which THE CHIEF JUSTICE, JUSTICE BREYER, and JUSTICE KAVANAUGH join.

Since 1925, the Bladensburg[, Maryland] Peace Cross (Cross) has stood as a tribute to 49 area soldiers who gave their lives in the First World War. Eighty-nine years after the dedication of the Cross, respondents filed this lawsuit, claiming that they are offended by the sight of the memorial on public land and that its presence there and the expenditure of public funds to maintain it violate the Establishment Clause of the First Amendment. To remedy this violation, they asked a federal court to order the relocation or demolition of the Cross or at least the removal of its arms. The Court of Appeals for the Fourth Circuit agreed that the memorial is unconstitutional and remanded for a determination of the proper remedy. We now reverse.

Although the cross has long been a preeminent Christian symbol, its use in the Bladensburg memorial has a special significance. After the First World War, the picture of row after row of plain white crosses marking the overseas graves of soldiers who had lost their lives in that horrible conflict was emblazoned on the minds of Americans at home, and the adoption of the cross as the Bladensburg memorial must be viewed in that historical context. For nearly a century, the Bladensburg Cross has expressed the community's grief at the loss of the young men who perished, its thanks for their sacrifice, and its dedication to the ideals for which they fought. It has become a prominent community landmark, and its removal or radical alteration at this date would be seen by many not as a neutral act but as the manifestation of "a hostility toward religion that has no place in our Establishment Clause traditions." And contrary to respondents' intimations, there is no evidence of discriminatory intent in the selection of the design of the memorial or the decision of a Maryland commission to maintain it. The Religion Clauses of the Constitution aim to foster a society in which people of all beliefs can live together harmoniously, and the presence of the Bladensburg Cross on the land where it has stood for so many years is fully consistent with that aim.

[The Court recounted the history of the cross and the recent litigation. It noted that the Fourth Circuit Court of Appeals, applying the *Lemon* test, found that there was a secular purpose, but concluded that it had the effect of advancing religion.]

II.A. The Establishment Clause of the First Amendment provides that "Congress shall make no law respecting an establishment of religion." While the concept of a formally established church is straightforward, pinning down the meaning of a "law respecting an establishment of religion" has proved to be a vexing problem. Prior to the Court's decision in *Everson v. Board of Ed. of Ewing*, the Establishment Clause was applied only to the Federal Government, and few cases involving this provision came before the Court. After *Everson* recognized the incorporation of the Clause, however, the Court faced a steady stream of difficult and controversial Establishment Clause issues, ranging from Bible reading and prayer in the public schools, to Sunday closing laws, to state subsidies for church-related schools or the parents of students attending those schools. After grappling with such cases for more than 20 years, *Lemon* ambitiously attempted to distill from the Court's existing case law a test that would bring order and predictability to Establishment Clause decisionmaking. That test . . . called on courts to examine the purposes and effects of a challenged government action, as well as any entanglement with religion that it might entail. The Court later elaborated that the "effect[s]" of a challenged action should be assessed by asking whether a "reasonable observer" would conclude that the action constituted an "endorsement" of religion.

If the *Lemon* Court thought that its test would provide a framework for all future Establishment Clause decisions, its expectation has not been met. In many cases, this Court has either expressly declined to apply the test or has simply ignored it.

This pattern is a testament to the *Lemon* test's shortcomings. As Establishment Clause cases involving a great array of laws and practices came to the Court, it became more and more apparent that the *Lemon* test could not resolve them. It could not "explain the Establishment Clause's tolerance, for example, of the prayers that open legislative meetings, . . . certain references to, and invocations of, the Deity in the public words of public officials; the public references to God on coins, decrees, and buildings; or the attention paid to the religious objectives of certain holidays, including Thanksgiving." The test has been harshly criticized by Members of this Court, lamented by lower court judges and questioned by a diverse roster of scholars.

For at least four reasons, the *Lemon* test presents particularly daunting problems in cases, including the one now before us, that involve the use, for ceremonial, celebratory, or commemorative purposes, of words or symbols with religious associations. Together, these considerations counsel against efforts to evaluate such cases under *Lemon* and toward application of a presumption of constitutionality for longstanding monuments, symbols, and practices.

B. *First*, these cases often concern monuments, symbols, or practices that were first established long ago, and in such cases, identifying their original purpose or purposes may be especially difficult. In *Salazar v. Buono*, for example, we dealt with a cross that a small group of World War I veterans had put up at a remote spot in the Mojave Desert more than seven decades earlier. The record contained virtually no direct evidence regarding the specific motivations of these men. . . .

Second, as time goes by, the purposes associated with an established monument, symbol, or practice often multiply. Take the example of Ten Commandments monuments, the subject we addressed in *Van Orden* and *McCreary County v. American Civil Liberties Union of Ky.* For believing Jews and Christians, the Ten Commandments are the word of God handed down to Moses on Mount Sinai, but the image of the Ten Commandments has also been used to convey other meanings. They have historical significance as one of the foundations of our legal system, and for largely that reason, they are depicted in the marble frieze in our courtroom and in other prominent public buildings in our Nation's capital. In *Van Orden* and *McCreary*, no Member of the Court thought that these depictions are unconstitutional.

Just as depictions of the Ten Commandments in these public buildings were intended to serve secular purposes, the litigation in *Van Orden* and *McCreary* showed that secular motivations played a part in the proliferation of Ten Commandments monuments in the 1950s. In 1946, Minnesota Judge E. J. Ruegemer proposed that the Ten Commandments be widely disseminated as a way of combating juvenile delinquency. With this prompting, the Fraternal Order of the Eagles began distributing paper copies of the Ten Commandments to churches, school groups, courts, and government offices. . . . At the same time, Cecil B. DeMille was filming The Ten Commandments. He learned of

Judge Ruegemer's campaign, and the two collaborated, deciding that the Commandments should be carved on stone tablets and that DeMille would make arrangements with the Eagles to help pay for them, thus simultaneously promoting his film and public awareness of the Decalogue. Not only did DeMille and Judge Ruegemer have different purposes, but the motivations of those who accepted the monuments and those responsible for maintaining them may also have differed. . . .

Third, just as the purpose for maintaining a monument, symbol, or practice may evolve, "[t]he 'message' conveyed . . . may change over time." Consider, for example, the message of the Statue of Liberty, which began as a monument to the solidarity and friendship between France and the United States and only decades later came to be seen "as a beacon welcoming immigrants to a land of freedom."

With sufficient time, religiously expressive monuments, symbols, and practices can become embedded features of a community's landscape and identity. The community may come to value them without necessarily embracing their religious roots. The recent tragic fire at Notre Dame in Paris provides a striking example. Although the French Republic rigorously enforces a secular public square, the cathedral remains a symbol of national importance to the religious and nonreligious alike. . . .

In the same way, consider the many cities and towns across the United States that bear religious names. Religion undoubtedly motivated those who named Bethlehem, Pennsylvania; Las Cruces, New Mexico; Providence, Rhode Island; Corpus Christi, Texas; Nephi, Utah, and the countless other places in our country with names that are rooted in religion. Yet few would argue that this history requires that these names be erased from the map. . . .

Fourth, when time's passage imbues a religiously expressive monument, symbol, or practice with this kind of familiarity and historical significance, removing it may no longer appear neutral, especially to the local community for which it has taken on particular meaning. A government that roams the land, tearing down monuments with religious symbolism and scrubbing away any reference to the divine will strike many as aggressively hostile to religion. Militantly secular regimes have carried out such projects in the past, and for those with a knowledge of history, the image of monuments being taken down will be evocative, disturbing, and divisive.

These four considerations show that retaining established, religiously expressive monuments, symbols, and practices is quite different from erecting or adopting new ones. The passage of time gives rise to a strong presumption of constitutionality.

C. The role of the cross in World War I memorials is illustrative of each of the four preceding considerations. Immediately following the war, "[c]ommunities across America built memorials to commemorate those who had served the nation in the struggle to make the world safe for democracy." Although not all of these communities included a cross in their memorials, the cross had become a symbol closely linked to the war. . . .

This is not to say that the cross's association with the war was the sole or dominant motivation for the inclusion of the symbol in every World War I memorial that features it. But today, it is all but impossible to tell whether that was so. . . .

Even the AHA recognizes that there are instances in which a war memorial in the form of a cross is unobjectionable. The AHA is not offended by the sight of the Argonne Cross or the Canadian Cross of Sacrifice, both Latin crosses commemorating World War I that rest on public grounds in Arlington National Cemetery. The difference, according to the AHA, is that their location in a cemetery gives them a closer association with individual gravestones and interred soldiers.

But a memorial's placement in a cemetery is not necessary to create such a connection. . . . Whether in a cemetery or a city park, a World War I cross remains a memorial to the fallen.

Similar reasoning applies to other memorials and monuments honoring important figures in our Nation's history. When faith was important to the person whose life is commemorated, it is natural to include a symbolic reference to faith in the design of the memorial. For example, many memorials for Dr. Martin Luther King, Jr., make reference to his faith. . . . These monuments honor men and women who have played an important role in the history of our country, and where religious symbols are included in the monuments, their presence acknowledges the centrality of faith to those whose lives are commemorated.

Finally, as World War I monuments have endured through the years and become a familiar part of the physical and cultural landscape, requiring their removal would not be viewed by many as a neutral act. And an alteration like the one entertained by the Fourth Circuit—amputating the arms of the Cross—would be seen by many as profoundly disrespectful. [A] campaign to obliterate items with religious associations may evidence hostility to religion even if those religious associations are no longer in the forefront.

For example, few would say that the State of California is attempting to convey a religious message by retaining the names given to many of the State's cities by their original Spanish settlers—San Diego, Los Angeles, Santa Barbara, San Jose, San Francisco, etc. But it would be something else entirely if the State undertook to change all those names. Much the same is true about monuments to soldiers who sacrificed their lives for this country more than a century ago.

D. While the *Lemon* Court ambitiously attempted to find a grand unified theory of the Establishment Clause, in later cases, we have taken a more modest approach that focuses on the particular issue at hand and looks to history for guidance. Our cases involving prayer before a legislative session are an example.

[Justice Alito noted that in both *Marsh v. Chambers* and *Town of Greece v. Galloway*, the Court upheld the practice of beginning a legislative assembly and a town meeting, respectively, and in both cases, the Court ignored *Lemon*.]

We reached these results even though it was clear, as stressed by the *Marsh* dissent, that prayer is by definition religious. . . .

[Justice Alito then described the history of opening legislative sessions with prayer, which dated back to the First Congres, and included Roman Catholic, Protestant, and Jewish clergy. "Since then, Congress has welcomed guest chaplains from a variety of faiths, including Islam, Hinduism, Buddhism, and Native American religions." And though lacking a similar provenance, the prayer opening the town council meeting in *Greece,* the Court concluded, " 'fi[t] within the tradition long followed in Congress and the state legislatures.' "]

The practice begun by the First Congress stands out as an example of respect and tolerance for differing views, an honest endeavor to achieve inclusivity and nondiscrimination, and a recognition of the important role that religion plays in the lives of many Americans. Where categories of monuments, symbols, and practices with a longstanding history follow in that tradition, they are likewise constitutional.

III. Applying these principles, we conclude that the Bladensburg Cross does not violate the Establishment Clause.

As we have explained, the Bladensburg Cross carries special significance in commemorating World War I. Due in large part to the image of the simple wooden crosses that originally marked the graves of American soldiers killed in the war, the cross became a symbol of their sacrifice, and the design of the Bladensburg Cross must be understood in light of that background. That the cross originated as a Christian symbol and retains that meaning in many contexts does not change the fact that the symbol took on an added secular meaning when used in World War I memorials.

[W]ith the passage of time, it has acquired historical importance. It reminds the people of Bladensburg and surrounding areas of the deeds of their predecessors and of the sacrifices they made in a war fought in the name of democracy. As long as it is retained in its original place and form, it speaks as well of the community that erected the monument nearly a century ago and has maintained it ever since. . . .

The monument would not serve that role if its design had deliberately disrespected area soldiers who perished in World War I. More than 3,500 Jewish soldiers gave their lives for the United States in that conflict, and some have wondered whether the names of any Jewish soldiers from the area were deliberately left off the list on the memorial or whether the names of any Jewish soldiers were included on the Cross against the wishes of their families. There is no evidence that either thing was done, and we do know that one of the local American Legion leaders responsible for the Cross's construction was a Jewish veteran.

The AHA's brief strains to connect the Bladensburg Cross and even the American Legion with anti-Semitism and the Ku Klux Klan, but the AHA's disparaging intimations have no evidentiary support. [In fact, the] Bladensburg Cross memorial included the names of both Black and White soldiers who had given their lives in the war; and despite the fact that Catholics and Baptists at that time were not exactly in the habit of participating together in ecumenical services, the ceremony dedicating the Cross began with an invocation by a Catholic priest and ended with a benediction by a Baptist pastor. . . .

Finally, it is surely relevant that the monument commemorates the death of particular individuals. It is natural and appropriate for those seeking to honor the deceased to invoke the symbols that signify what death meant for those who are memorialized. In some circumstances, the exclusion of any such recognition would make a memorial incomplete. This well explains why Holocaust memorials invariably include Stars of David or other symbols of Judaism. . . . And this is why the memorial for soldiers from the Bladensburg community features the cross — the same symbol that marks the graves of so many of their comrades near the battlefields where they fell

IV. The cross is undoubtedly a Christian symbol, but that fact should not blind us to everything else that the Bladensburg Cross has come to represent. For some, that monument is a symbolic resting place for ancestors who never returned home. For others, it is a place for the community to gather and honor all veterans and their sacrifices for our Nation. For others still, it is a historical landmark. For many of these people, destroying or defacing the Cross that has stood undisturbed for nearly a century would not be neutral and would not further the ideals of respect and tolerance embodied in the First Amendment. For all these reasons, the Cross does not offend the Constitution.

* * *

We reverse the judgment of the Court of Appeals for the Fourth Circuit and remand the cases for further proceedings.

It is so ordered.

Justice Breyer, with whom Justice Kagan joins, concurring.

I have long maintained that there is no single formula for resolving Establishment Clause challenges. The Court must instead consider each case in light of the basic purposes that the Religion Clauses were meant to serve: assuring religious liberty and tolerance for all, avoiding religiously based social conflict, and maintaining that separation of church and state that allows each to flourish in its "separate spher[e]."

I agree with the Court that allowing the State of Maryland to display and maintain the Peace Cross poses no threat to those ends. The Court's opinion eloquently explains why that is so: The Latin cross is uniquely associated with the fallen soldiers of World War I; the organizers of the Peace Cross acted with the undeniably secular motive of commemorating local soldiers; no evidence suggests that they sought to disparage or exclude any religious group; the secular values inscribed on the Cross and its place among other memorials strengthen its message of patriotism and commemoration; and, finally, the Cross has stood on the same land for 94 years, generating no controversy in the community until this lawsuit was filed. [A]s the Court explains, ordering its removal or alteration at this late date would signal "a hostility toward religion that has no place in our Establishment Clause traditions." . . .

JUSTICE KAVANAUGH, concurring.

I join the Court's eloquent and persuasive opinion in full. I write separately to emphasize two points

I. Consistent with the Court's case law, the Court today applies a history and tradition test in examining and upholding the constitutionality of the Bladensburg Cross. . . .

As this case again demonstrates, this Court no longer applies the old test articulated in *Lemon* v. *Kurtzman* . . . . If *Lemon* guided this Court's understanding of the Establishment Clause, then many of the Court's Establishment Clause cases over the last 48 years would have been decided differently . . . .

[Justice Kavanaugh's opinion then proceeds to identify different categories of Establishment Clause cases and argues that many in those categories would have come out the other way had the *Lemon* test been employed.]

II. [I] have deep respect for the plaintiffs' sincere objections to seeing the cross on public land. I have great respect for the Jewish war veterans who in an *amicus* brief say that the cross on public land sends a message of exclusion. I recognize their sense of distress and alienation. Moreover, I fully understand the deeply religious nature of the cross. It would demean both believers and nonbelievers to say that the cross is not religious, or not all that religious. A case like this is difficult because it represents a clash of genuine and important interests. Applying our precedents, we uphold the constitutionality of the cross. In doing so, it is appropriate to also restate this bedrock constitutional principle: All citizens are equally American, no matter what religion they are, or if they have no religion at all.

The conclusion that the cross does not violate the Establishment Clause does not necessarily mean that those who object to it have no other recourse. The Court's ruling *allows* the State to maintain the cross on public land. The Court's ruling does not *require* the State to maintain the cross on public land. The Maryland Legislature could enact new laws requiring removal of the cross or transfer of the land. The Maryland Governor or other state or local executive officers may have authority to do so under current Maryland law. And if not, the legislature could enact new laws to authorize such executive action. The Maryland Constitution, as interpreted by the Maryland Court of Appeals, may speak to this question. And if not, the people of Maryland can amend the State Constitution.

Those alternative avenues of relief illustrate a fundamental feature of our constitutional structure: This Court is not the *only* guardian of individual rights in America. . . .

JUSTICE KAGAN, concurring in part.

. . . Although I agree that rigid application of the *Lemon* test does not solve every Establishment Clause problem, I think that test's focus on purposes and effects is crucial in evaluating government action in this sphere—as this very suit shows. I therefore do not join Part II–A. I do not join Part II–D out of perhaps an excess of caution. Although I too "look[] to history for guidance," I prefer at least for now to do so case-by-case, rather than to sign on to any broader statements about history's role in Establishment Clause analysis. . . .

[A concurring opinion of Justice Thomas is omitted.]

[Justice Gorsuch wrote an opining concurring in judgment; he argued that the plaintiffs lacked standing to bring the case. Specifically, he argued they failed to prove injury-in-fact.]

JUSTICE GINSBURG, with whom JUSTICE SOTOMAYOR joins, dissenting.

. . . Decades ago, this Court recognized that the Establishment Clause of the First Amendment to the Constitution demands governmental neutrality among religious faiths, and between religion and nonreligion. Numerous times since, the Court has reaffirmed the Constitution's commitment to neutrality. Today the Court erodes that neutrality commitment, diminishing precedent designed to preserve individual liberty and civic harmony in favor of a "presumption of constitutionality for longstanding monuments, symbols, and practices."

The Latin cross is the foremost symbol of the Christian faith, embodying the "central theological claim of Christianity: that the son of God died on the cross, that he rose from the dead, and that his death and resurrection offer the possibility of eternal life." Precisely because the cross symbolizes these sectarian beliefs, it is a common marker for the graves of Christian soldiers. For the same reason, using the cross as a war memorial does not transform it into a secular symbol . . . . Just as a Star of David is not suitable to honor Christians who died serving their country, so a cross is not suitable to honor those of other faiths who died defending their nation. Soldiers of all faiths "are united by their love of country, but they are not united by the cross."

By maintaining the Peace Cross on a public highway, the Commission elevates Christianity over other faiths, and religion over nonreligion. Memorializing the service of American soldiers is an "admirable and unquestionably secular" objective. But the Commission does not serve that objective by displaying a symbol that bears "a starkly sectarian message."

NOTES AND PROBLEM

1. What Is the Scope of *AHA*? Does the Court mean to fashion a new test to replace *Lemon* in all Establishment Clause cases or is this approach restricted to cases involving "longstanding monuments, symbols, and practices" involving "the use, for ceremonial, celebratory, or commemorative purpose, of words or symbols with religious associations"? Does it, for example, apply to future cases involving prayer before public school graduations (*Lee v. Weisman*) or athletic contests (*Santa Fe Independent School District v. Doe*)? Both have fairly established historical pedigrees. A case could be made that both are recited not out of abundance of piety but rather as a means of establishing the solemnity of graduation or a kind of atavistic appeal for players' safety — like rubbing a rabbit's foot or knocking on wood.

2. What Is the Test in *AHA*? Whatever its intended scope, what is the test that courts will hereafter apply? Justice Alito lists four reasons *Lemon* has proven unsatisfactory in longstanding religious symbol cases — (1) difficulty of establishing past motive of the initial adopters; (2) purposes associated with a symbol can multiply and represent secular principles; (3) the purpose for retaining a symbol can evolve over time; and (4) when a monument, symbol, or practice becomes embedded in a community's identity, removal "may no longer appear to be neutral" — but it is unclear what role (if any) those play in the presumption of constitutionality longstanding monuments are said to enjoy. Later in the opinion, moreover, Justice Alito mentions that there no evidence suggesting that the cross was adopted to exclude or disparage members of other religions. Do those statements imply that *were* there such evidence, it would be sufficient to overcome the presumption of constitutionality? What if the discriminatory roots of the monument had been, until litigation, lost to history?

3. The Nature of the Test. Do you agree with Justice Kavanaugh that the Court adopted a "history and tradition" test for these monuments or are Justices Breyer and Kagan closer to the mark when they suggest that the Court here is simply considering that history and tradition in addition to a number of other factors, including whether citizens have complained about the monument in the past?

4. Is the Test Symmetrical? If longstanding monuments — at least those whose erection is untainted by bigotry or discrimination — are presumed constitutional, what about new monuments like the installation of the Ten Commandments in the *McCreary County* case? Do recent establishments of monuments, ceremonies, or symbols with close associations with a particular religion come with a presumption of *un*constitutionality? Is *Lemon* more easily applicable in such cases because the proximity of the decision to establish or install the symbol or monument make the "secular purpose" requirement easier to evaluate?

5. Problem. If a plaintiff with standing ever successfully brings suit challenging the practice of reciting the Pledge of Allegiance in public schools using the phrase "One Nation under God," does *AHA* apply in such a case? Would it help or hurt the plaintiff? Is it relevant to either party that the phrase was added in 1954 to provide a contrast between the United States and the officially atheistic Soviet Union?

Chapter 11

State Action and the Power to Enforce Constitutional Rights

A. State Action

1. The Public Function Doctrine

Page 1251: Insert at the end of note 1:

   Manhattan Community Access Corp. v. Halleck, 139 S. Ct. 1921 (2019). Two contributors to a private nonprofit corporation, the Manhattan Neighborhood Network (MNN), that ran public access channels on Manhattan's cable system were suspended after the MNN received complaints from its employees alleging harassment. The contributors then filed suit, claiming that the suspension violated their First Amendment rights. The Court concluded that "operation of public access channels on a cable system is not a traditional, exclusive public function." Further, it held that "a private entity such as MNN who opens its property for speech by others is not transformed by that fact alone into a state actor. In operating the public access channels, MNN is a private actor, not a state actor, and MNN therefore is not subject to First Amendment constraints on its editorial discretion."

Chapter 12

The Right to Keep and Bear Arms

Page 1327: Insert after note 7:

NEW YORK STATE RIFLE & PISTOL ASSOCIATION, INC. v. BRUEN
Supreme Court of the United States
2022 WL 2251305

JUSTICE THOMAS delivered the opinion of the Court.

[In order to carry a concealed weapon in New York for self-defense, you must possess a permit issued by a state licensing official; to obtain such a permit, you must demonstrate that "proper cause" exists for issuance. If an applicant cannot demonstrate proper cause, the applicant "can receive only a 'restricted' license for public carry, which allows him to carry a firearm for a limited purpose, such as hunting, target shooting, or employment." New York courts have construed "proper cause" to mean a need that is distinguishable from that of the public at large. Merely living in a high-crime area, for example, did not constitute proper cause. "New York courts generally require evidence of 'particular threats, attacks or other extraordinary danger to personal safety.'" Judicial review of a denial is limited to an inquiry into whether the denial was arbitrary and capricious; if there is a rational basis for the denial, it will be upheld. By contrast forty-three states are now "shall issue" states "where authorities must issue concealed-carry licenses whenever applicants satisfy certain threshold requirements, without granting licensing officials discretion to deny licenses based on a perceived lack of need or suitability."

The petitioners, Brandon Koch and Robert Nash, both members of the New York State Rifle and Pistol Association, applied for unrestricted public carry licenses citing self-defense as their reason. Both instead received restricted carry permits limiting them to carrying for hunting and target shooting. Both later sought to have the restrictions removed; Nash cited a spate of robberies in his neighbor as the reason, Koch "his extensive experience in safely handling firearms. Both requests were rejected, though "the officer permitted Koch to 'carry to and from work.'" They filed suit, claiming that the "proper cause" requirement infringed their Second Amendment rights (as incorporated by the Fourteenth Amendment.]

II. In *Heller* and *McDonald*, we held that the Second and Fourteenth Amendments protect an individual right to keep and bear arms for self-defense. In doing so, we held unconstitutional two laws that prohibited the possession and use of handguns in the home. In the years since, the Courts of Appeals have coalesced around a "two-step" framework for analyzing Second Amendment challenges that combines history with means-end scrutiny.

Today, we decline to adopt that two-part approach. In keeping with *Heller*, we hold that when the Second Amendment's plain text covers an individual's conduct, the Constitution presumptively protects that conduct. To justify its regulation, the government may not simply posit that the regulation promotes an important interest. Rather, the government must demonstrate that the regulation is consistent with this Nation's historical tradition of firearm regulation. Only if a firearm regulation is consistent with this Nation's historical tradition may a court conclude that the individual's conduct falls outside the Second Amendment's "unqualified command."

[Justice Thomas described the Courts of Appeals approach. "At the first step, the government may justify its regulation by 'establish[ing] that the challenged law regulates activity falling outside the scope of the right as originally understood.' If the government can prove that the regulated conduct falls beyond the Amendment's original scope, 'then the analysis can stop there; the regulated activity is categorically unprotected.'" Next, "courts often analyze 'how close the law comes to the core of the Second Amendment right and the severity of the law's burden on that right.'" If it is close to the core, and the burden is severe then the courts have applied strict scrutiny; otherwise, intermediate scrutiny is employed.]

II.B. Despite the popularity of this two-step approach, it is one step too many. Step one of the predominant framework is broadly consistent with *Heller*, which demands a test rooted in the Second Amendment's text, as informed by history. But *Heller* and *McDonald* do not support applying means-end scrutiny in the Second Amendment context. Instead, the government must affirmatively prove that its firearms regulation is part of the historical tradition that delimits the outer bounds of the right to keep and bear arms. . . .

2. [T]he Courts of Appeals' second step is inconsistent with *Heller*'s historical approach and its rejection of means-end scrutiny. We reiterate that the standard for applying the Second Amendment is as follows: When the Second Amendment's plain text covers an individual's conduct, the Constitution presumptively protects that conduct. The government must then justify its regulation by demonstrating that it is consistent with the Nation's historical tradition of firearm regulation. Only then may a court conclude that the individual's conduct falls outside the Second Amendment's "unqualified command." . . .

III. Having made the constitutional standard endorsed in *Heller* more explicit, we now apply that standard to New York's proper-cause requirement.

A. It is undisputed that petitioners Koch and Nash—two ordinary, law-abiding, adult citizens—are part of "the people" whom the Second Amendment protects. Nor does any party dispute that handguns are weapons "in common use" today for self-defense. We therefore turn to whether the plain text of the Second Amendment protects Koch's and Nash's proposed course of conduct — carrying handguns publicly for self-defense.

We have little difficulty concluding that it does. Respondents do not dispute this. Nor could they. Nothing in the Second Amendment's text draws a home/ public distinction with respect to the right to keep and bear arms. As we explained in *Heller*, the "textual elements" of the Second Amendment's operative clause — "the right of the people to keep and bear Arms, shall not be infringed" — "guarantee the individual right to possess and carry weapons in case of confrontation." *Heller* further confirmed that the right to "bear arms" refers to the right to "wear, bear, or carry . . . upon the person or in the clothing or in a pocket, for the purpose . . . of being armed and ready for offensive or defensive action in a case of conflict with another person."

This definition of "bear" naturally encompasses public carry. Most gun owners do not wear a holstered pistol at their hip in their bedroom or while sitting at the dinner table. Although individuals often "keep" firearms in their home, at the ready for self-defense, most do not "bear" (*i.e.*, carry) them in the home beyond moments of actual confrontation. To confine the right to "bear" arms to the home would nullify half of the Second Amendment's operative protections.

Moreover, confining the right to "bear" arms to the home would make little sense given that self-defense is "the *central component* of the [Second Amendment] right itself." After all, the Second Amendment guarantees an "individual right to possess and carry weapons in case of confrontation,"

Although we remarked in *Heller* that the need for armed self-defense is perhaps "most acute" in the home, we did not suggest that the need was insignificant elsewhere. Many Americans hazard greater danger outside the home than in it. . . .

3. The Second Amendment's plain text thus presumptively guarantees petitioners Koch and Nash a right to "bear" arms in public for self-defense.

B. Conceding that the Second Amendment guarantees a general right to public carry, respondents instead claim that the Amendment "permits a State to condition handgun carrying in areas 'frequented by the general public' on a showing of a nonspeculative need for armed self-defense in those areas." To support that claim, the burden falls on respondents to show that New York's proper-cause requirement is consistent with this Nation's historical tradition of firearm regulation. Only if respondents carry that burden can they show that the pre-existing right codified in the Second Amendment, and made applicable to the States through the Fourteenth, does not protect petitioners' proposed course of conduct.

Respondents appeal to a variety of historical sources from the late 1200s to the early 1900s. We categorize these periods as follows: (1) medieval to early modern England; (2) the American Colonies and the early Republic; (3) antebellum America; (4) Reconstruction; and (5) the late-19th and early-20th centuries. . . .

1. [Justice Thomas began with a review of "English history and custom before the founding" and argued that many of the very earliest regulations were aimed at those who would ride armed intent on terrorizing the populace or breaching the peace. James I had banned small pistols ("dags"), but that was because he deemed them ineffective. In any event, Justice Thomas wrote, "James I's proclamation in 1616 'was the last one regarding civilians carrying dags,' 'After this the question faded without explanation.' So, by the time Englishmen began to arrive in America in the early 1600s, the public carry of handguns was no longer widely proscribed." After reviewing the history, Justice Thomas wrote that "we cannot conclude from this historical record that, by the time of the founding, English law would have justified restricting the right to publicly bear arms suited for self-defense only to those who demonstrate some special need for self-protection."]

2. Respondents next point us to the history of the Colonies and early Republic, but there is little evidence of an early American practice of regulating public carry by the general public. This should come as no surprise—English subjects founded the Colonies at about the time England had itself begun to eliminate restrictions on the ownership and use of handguns.

In the colonial era, respondents point to only three restrictions on public carry. For starters, we doubt that *three* colonial regulations could suffice to show a tradition of public-carry regulation. In any event, even looking at these laws on their own terms, we are not convinced that they regulated public carry akin to the New York law before us. . . .

Far from banning the carrying of any class of firearms, they merely codified the existing common-law offense of bearing arms to terrorize the people, as had the Statute of Northampton itself. For instance, the Massachusetts statute proscribed "go[ing] armed Offensively . . . in Fear or Affray" of the people, indicating that these laws were modeled after the Statute of Northampton to the extent that the statute would have been understood to limit public carry *in the late 1600s.* Moreover, it makes very little sense to read these statutes as banning the public carry of all firearms just a few years after Chief Justice Holt in *Sir John Knight's Case* indicated that the English common law did not do so.

Regardless, even if respondents' reading of these colonial statutes were correct, it would still do little to support restrictions on the public carry of handguns *today.* At most, respondents can show that colonial legislatures sometimes prohibited the carrying of "dangerous and unusual weapons"—a fact we already acknowledged in *Heller.* . . . [E]ven if these colonial laws prohibited the carrying of handguns because they were considered "dangerous and unusual weapons" in the 1690s, they provide no justification for laws restricting the public carry of weapons that are unquestionably in common use today.

The third statute . . . enacted in East New Jersey in 1686 . . . prohibited the concealed carry of "pocket pistol[s]" or other "unusual or unlawful weapons," and it further prohibited "planter[s]" from carrying all pistols unless in military service or, if "strangers," when traveling through the Province. . . . The law restricted only concealed carry, not all public carry, and its restrictions applied only to certain "unusual or unlawful weapons," including "pocket pistol[s]." . . . Moreover, the law prohibited only the *concealed* carry of pocket pistols; it presumably did not by its terms touch the open carry of larger, presumably more common pistols, except as to "planters." In colonial times, a "planter" was simply a farmer or plantation owner who settled new territory. While the reason behind this singular restriction is not entirely clear, planters may have been targeted because colonial-era East New Jersey was riven with "strife and excitement" between planters and the Colony's proprietors "respecting titles to the soil."

In any event, we cannot put meaningful weight on this solitary statute. First, although the "planter" restriction may have prohibited the public carry of pistols, it did not prohibit planters from carrying long guns for self-defense—including the popular musket and carbine. Second, it does not appear that the statute survived for very long. By 1694, East New Jersey provided that no slave "be permitted to carry any gun or pistol . . . into the woods, or plantations" unless their owner accompanied them. If slave-owning planters were prohibited from carrying pistols, it is hard to comprehend why slaves would have been able to carry them in the planter's presence. . .

Respondents next direct our attention to three late-18th-century and early-19th-century statutes, but each parallels the colonial statutes already discussed. . . .

A by-now-familiar thread runs through these three statutes: They prohibit bearing arms in a way that spreads "fear" or "terror" among the people. . . . Thus, all told, in the century leading up to the Second Amendment and in the first decade after its adoption, there is no historical basis for concluding that the pre-existing right enshrined in the Second Amendment permitted broad prohibitions on all forms of public carry.

3. Only after the ratification of the Second Amendment in 1791 did public-carry restrictions proliferate. Respondents rely heavily on these restrictions, which generally fell into three categories: common-law offenses, statutory prohibitions, and "surety" statutes. None of these restrictions imposed a substantial burden on public carry analogous to the burden created by New York's restrictive licensing regime.

Common-Law Offenses. As during the colonial and founding periods, the common-law offenses of "affray" or going armed "to the terror of the people" continued to impose some limits on firearm carry in the antebellum period. But as with the earlier periods, there is no evidence indicating that these common-law limitations impaired the right of the general population to peaceable public carry. . . .

Statutory Prohibitions. In the early to mid-19th century, some States began enacting laws that proscribed the concealed carry of pistols and other small weapons. As we recognized in *Heller*, "the majority of the 19th-century courts to consider the question held that [these] prohibitions on carrying concealed weapons were lawful under the Second Amendment or state analogues." Respondents unsurprisingly cite these statutes — and decisions upholding them — as evidence that States were historically free to ban public carry.

In fact, however, the history reveals a consensus that States could *not* ban public carry. Respondents' cited opinions agreed that concealed-carry prohibitions were constitutional only if they did not similarly prohibit *open* carry. That was true in [Alabama, Louisiana, and Kentucky. He also cited a Georgia case holding that a statute prohibiting the wearing or carrying of pistols was valid only insofar as it applied to the concealed carrying of weapons.]

Finally, we agree that Tennessee's prohibition on carrying "publicly or privately" any "belt or pocket pisto[l]," was, on its face, uniquely severe. That said, when the Tennessee Supreme Court addressed the constitutionality of a substantively identical successor provision, the court read this language to permit the public carry of larger, military-style pistols because any categorical prohibition on their carry would "violat[e] the constitutional right to keep arms."

All told, these antebellum state-court decisions evince a consensus view that States could not altogether prohibit the public carry of "arms" protected by the Second Amendment or state analogues.

Surety Statutes. In the mid-19th century, many jurisdictions began adopting surety statutes that required certain individuals to post bond before carrying weapons in public. Although respondents seize on these laws to justify the proper-cause restriction, their reliance on them is misplaced. These laws were not *bans* on public carry, and they typically targeted only those threatening to do harm. . . .

[U]nlike New York's regime, a showing of special need was required only *after* an individual was reasonably accused of intending to injure another or breach the peace. And, even then, proving special need simply avoided a fee rather than a ban. All told, therefore, "[u]nder surety laws . . . everyone started out with robust carrying rights" and only those reasonably accused were required to show a special need in order to avoid posting a bond. These antebellum special-need requirements "did not expand carrying for the responsible; it shrank burdens on carrying by the (allegedly) reckless." . . .

Besides, respondents offer little evidence that authorities ever enforced surety laws. The only recorded case that we know of involved a justice of the peace *declining* to require a surety, even when the complainant alleged that the arms-bearer " 'did threaten to beat, wou[n]d, mai[m], and kill' " him. And one scholar who canvassed 19th-century newspapers — which routinely reported on local judicial matters — found only a handful of other examples in Massachusetts and the District of Columbia, all involving black defendants who may have been targeted for selective or pretextual enforcement. That is surely too slender a reed on which to hang a historical tradition of restricting the right to public carry.

Respondents also argue that surety statutes were severe restrictions on firearms because the "reasonable cause to fear" standard was essentially *pro forma,* given that "merely carrying firearms in populous areas breached the peace" *per se*. But that is a counterintuitive reading of the language that the surety statutes actually used. If the mere carrying of handguns breached the peace, it would be odd to draft a surety statute requiring a complainant to demonstrate "reasonable cause to fear an injury, or breach of the peace," rather than a reasonable likelihood that the arms-bearer carried a covered weapon. After all, if it was the nature of the weapon rather than the manner of carry that was dispositive, then the "reasonable fear" requirement would be redundant.

Moreover, the overlapping scope of surety statutes and criminal statutes suggests that the former were not viewed as substantial restrictions on public carry. For example, when Massachusetts enacted its surety statute in 1836, it reaffirmed its 1794 criminal prohibition on "go[ing] armed offensively, to the terror of the people." And Massachusetts continued to criminalize the carrying of various "dangerous weapons" well after passing the 1836 surety statute. Similarly, Virginia had criminalized the concealed carry of pistols since 1838, nearly a decade before it enacted its surety statute. It is unlikely that these surety statutes constituted a "severe" restraint on public carry, let alone a restriction tantamount to a ban, when they were supplemented by direct criminal prohibitions on specific weapons and methods of carry.

To summarize: The historical evidence from antebellum America does demonstrate that *the manner* of public carry was subject to reasonable regulation. Under the common law, individuals could not carry deadly weapons in a manner likely to terrorize others. Similarly, although surety statutes did not directly restrict public carry, they did provide financial incentives for responsible arms carrying. Finally, States could lawfully eliminate one kind of public carry — concealed carry — so long as they left open the option to carry openly.

None of these historical limitations . . . operated to prevent law-abiding citizens with ordinary self-defense needs from carrying arms in public for that purpose.

4. Evidence from around the adoption of the Fourteenth Amendment also fails to support respondents' position. . . .

[Justice Thomas then recounts the Reconstruction-era debates over the Fourteenth Amendment and the extent to which the Framers of that amendment intended it, in part, to safeguard the right to keep and bear arms especially for newly freed slaves who found themselves subject to campaigns to disarm them in the former Confederate states. He acknowledged that "even during Reconstruction the right to keep and bear arms had limits. But those limits were consistent with a right of the public to peaceably carry handguns for self-defense." And even those "Reconstruction-era state regulations [were] the kinds of public-carry restrictions that had been commonplace in the early 19th century," i.e., prohibitions on going armed in public to terrify the populace and surety statutes.]

Respondents and the United States, however, direct our attention primarily to two late-19th-century cases in Texas. In 1871, Texas law forbade anyone from "carrying on or about his person . . . any pistol . . . unless he has reasonable grounds for fearing an unlawful attack on his person." The Texas Supreme Court upheld that restriction [reasoning] that the Second Amendment, and the State's constitutional analogue, protected only those arms "as are useful and proper to an armed militia," including holster pistols, but not other kinds of handguns. . . .

Four years later, . . . the Texas Supreme Court modified its analysis [reinterpreting] Texas' State Constitution to protect not only military-style weapons but rather all arms "as are commonly kept, according to the customs of the people, and are appropriate for open and manly use in self-defense." On that understanding, the court recognized that, in addition to "holster pistol[s]," the right to bear arms covered the carry of "such pistols at least as are not adapted to being carried concealed." Nonetheless, after expanding the scope of firearms that warranted state constitutional protection, [the court] held that requiring any pistol-bearer to have " 'reasonable grounds fearing an unlawful attack on [one's] person' " was a "legitimate and highly proper" regulation of handgun carriage.

We acknowledge that the Texas cases support New York's proper-cause requirement, which one can analogize to Texas' "reasonable grounds" standard. But the Texas statute . . . are outliers. [O]nly one other State, West Virginia, adopted a similar public-carry statute before 1900. . . .

In the end, while we recognize the support that postbellum Texas provides for respondents' view, we will not give disproportionate weight to a single state statute and a pair of state-court decisions. . . .

5. Finally, respondents point to the slight uptick in gun regulation during the late-19th century—principally in the Western Territories. As we suggested in *Heller*, however, late-19th-century evidence cannot provide much insight into the meaning of the Second Amendment when it contradicts earlier evidence. . . .

The vast majority of the statutes that respondents invoke come from the Western Territories. Two Territories prohibited the carry of pistols in towns, cities, and villages, but seemingly permitted the carry of rifles and other long guns everywhere. Two others prohibited the carry of *all* firearms in towns, cities, and villages, including long guns. And one Territory completely prohibited public carry of pistols *everywhere*, but allowed the carry of "shot-guns or rifles" for certain purposes.

These territorial restrictions fail to justify New York's proper-cause requirement for several reasons. First, the bare existence of these localized restrictions cannot overcome the overwhelming evidence of an otherwise enduring American tradition permitting public carry. . . . These territorial "legislative improvisations," which conflict with the Nation's earlier approach to firearm regulation, are most unlikely to reflect "the origins and continuing significance of the Second Amendment" and we do not consider them "instructive."

The exceptional nature of these western restrictions is all the more apparent when one considers the miniscule territorial populations who would have lived under them. [According to the 1890 census] roughly 62 million people lived in the United States at that time. Arizona, Idaho, New Mexico, Oklahoma, and

Wyoming [the territories that limited public carrying] combined to account for only 420,000 of those inhabitants—about two-thirds of 1% of the population. [W]e will not stake our interpretation on a handful of temporary territorial laws that were enacted nearly a century after the Second Amendment's adoption, governed less than 1% of the American population, and also "contradic[t] the overwhelming weight" of other, more contemporaneous historical evidence.

Second, because these territorial laws were rarely subject to judicial scrutiny, we do not know the basis of their perceived legality. . . .

Absent any evidence explaining *why* these unprecedented prohibitions on *all* public carry were understood to comport with the Second Amendment, we fail to see how they inform "the origins and continuing significance of the Amendment." . . .

Finally, these territorial restrictions deserve little weight because they were— consistent with the transitory nature of territorial government—short lived. Some were held unconstitutional shortly after passage. . . .

Beyond these Territories, respondents identify one Western State—Kansas— that instructed cities with more than 15,000 inhabitants to pass ordinances prohibiting the public carry of firearms. . . . Although other Kansas cities may also have restricted public carry unilaterally, the lone late-19th-century state law respondents identify does not prove that Kansas meaningfully restricted public carry, let alone demonstrate a broad tradition of States doing so.

* * *

At the end of this long journey through the Anglo-American history of public carry, we conclude that respondents have not met their burden to identify an American tradition justifying the State's proper-cause requirement. The Second Amendment guaranteed to "all Americans" the right to bear commonly used arms in public subject to certain reasonable, well-defined restrictions. Those restrictions . . . limited the intent for which one could carry arms, the manner by which one carried arms, or the exceptional circumstances under which one could not carry arms, such as before justices of the peace and other government officials. Apart from a few late-19th-century outlier jurisdictions, American governments simply have not broadly prohibited the public carry of commonly used firearms for personal defense. Nor, subject to a few late-in-time outliers, have American governments required law-abiding, responsible citizens to "demonstrate a special need for self-protection distinguishable from that of the general community" in order to carry arms in public.

IV. The constitutional right to bear arms in public for self-defense is not "a second-class right, subject to an entirely different body of rules than the other Bill of Rights guarantees." We know of no other constitutional right that an individual may exercise only after demonstrating to government officers some special need. That is not how the First Amendment works when it comes to unpopular speech or the free exercise of religion. It is not how the Sixth Amendment works when it comes to a defendant's right to confront the witnesses against him. And it is not how the Second Amendment works when it comes to public carry for self-defense.

New York's proper-cause requirement violates the Fourteenth Amendment in that it prevents law-abiding citizens with ordinary self-defense needs from exercising their right to keep and bear arms. We therefore reverse the judgment of the Court of Appeals and remand the case for further proceedings consistent with this opinion.

It is so ordered.

[A concurring opinion by Justice Alito is omitted.]

JUSTICE KAVANAUGH, with whom THE CHIEF JUSTICE joins, concurring. . . .

I join the Court's opinion, and I write separately to underscore two important points about the limits of the Court's decision.

First, the Court's decision does not prohibit States from imposing licensing requirements for carrying a handgun for self-defense. In particular, the Court's decision does not affect the existing licensing regimes—known as "shall-issue" regimes—that are employed in 43 States. . . .

As the Court explains, New York's outlier may-issue regime is constitutionally problematic because it grants open-ended discretion to licensing officials and authorizes licenses only for those applicants who can show some special need apart from self-defense. Those features of New York's regime—the unchanneled discretion for licensing officials and the special-need requirement—in effect deny the right to carry handguns for self-defense to many "ordinary, law-abiding citizens." . . .

By contrast, 43 States employ objective shall-issue licensing regimes. Those shall-issue regimes may require a license applicant to undergo fingerprinting, a background check, a mental health records check, and training in firearms handling and in laws regarding the use of force, among other possible requirements. Unlike New York's may-issue regime, those shall-issue regimes do not grant open-ended discretion to licensing officials and do not require a showing of some special need apart from self-defense. . . .

Going forward, therefore, the 43 States that employ objective shall-issue licensing regimes for carrying handguns for self-defense may continue to do so. Likewise, the 6 States including New York potentially affected by today's decision may continue to require licenses for carrying handguns for self-defense so long as those States employ objective licensing requirements like those used by the 43 shall-issue States.

Second, as *Heller* and *McDonald* established and the Court today again explains, the Second Amendment "is neither a regulatory straightjacket nor a regulatory blank check." Properly interpreted, the Second Amendment allows a "variety" of gun regulations. . . .

[A concurring opinion by Justice Barrett is omitted.]

JUSTICE BREYER, with whom JUSTICE SOTOMAYOR and JUSTICE KAGAN join, dissenting. . . .

Many States have tried to address some of the dangers of gun violence just described by passing laws that limit, in various ways, who may purchase, carry, or use firearms of different kinds. The Court today severely burdens States' efforts to do so. It invokes the Second Amendment to strike down a New York law regulating the public carriage of concealed handguns. In my view, that decision rests upon several serious mistakes.

First, the Court decides this case on the basis of the pleadings, without the benefit of discovery or an evidentiary record. As a result, it may well rest its decision on a mistaken understanding of how New York's law operates in practice. Second, the Court wrongly limits its analysis to focus nearly exclusively on history. It refuses to consider the government interests that justify a challenged gun regulation, regardless of how compelling those interests may be. The Constitution contains no such limitation, and neither do our precedents. Third, the Court itself demonstrates the practical problems with its history-only approach. In applying that approach to New York's law, the Court fails to correctly identify and analyze the relevant historical facts. Only by ignoring an abundance of historical evidence supporting regulations restricting the public carriage of firearms can the Court conclude that New York's law is not "consistent with the Nation's historical tradition of firearm regulation."

In my view, when courts interpret the Second Amendment, it is constitutionally proper, indeed often necessary, for them to consider the serious dangers and consequences of gun violence that lead States to regulate firearms. The Second Circuit has done so and has held that New York's law does not violate the Second Amendment. I would affirm that holding. At a minimum, I would not strike down the law based only on the pleadings . . . without first allowing for the development of an evidentiary record and without considering the State's compelling interest in preventing gun violence. I respectfully dissent.

I. [Justice Breyer began his dissent with a catalogue of the ways in which gun violence remains an endemic problem in the United States. In addition to suicides, homicides, and accidental shootings, there are the problems of mass shootings, road rage incidents, armed protests that turn violent, and dangers to police that the proliferation of an armed citizenry pose. He concluded:]

These are just some examples of the dangers that firearms pose. There is, of course, another side to the story. I am not simply saying that "guns are bad." Some Americans use guns for legitimate purposes, such as sport (*e.g.,* hunting or target shooting), certain types of employment (*e.g.,* as a private security guard), or self-defense. Balancing these lawful uses against the dangers of firearms is primarily the responsibility of elected bodies, such as legislatures. It requires consideration of facts, statistics, expert opinions, predictive judgments, relevant values, and a host of other circumstances, which together make decisions about how, when, and where to regulate guns more appropriately legislative work. That consideration counsels modesty and restraint on the part of judges when they interpret and apply the Second Amendment. . . .

II.B. In describing New York's law, the Court . . . suggests that New York's licensing regime gives licensing officers too much discretion and provides too "limited" judicial review of their decisions; that the proper cause standard is too "demanding"; and that these features make New York an outlier compared to the "vast majority of States," But on what evidence does the Court base these characterizations? Recall that this case comes to us at the pleading stage. The parties have not had an opportunity to conduct discovery, and no evidentiary hearings have been held to develop the record. Thus, at this point, there is no record to support the Court's negative characterizations, as we know very little about how the law has actually been applied on the ground. . . .

First, the Court says that New York gives licensing officers too much discretion and "leaves applicants little recourse if their local licensing officer denies a permit." But there is nothing unusual about broad statutory language that can be given more specific content by judicial interpretation. Nor is there anything unusual or inadequate about subjecting licensing officers' decisions to arbitrary-and-capricious review. Judges routinely apply that standard, for example, to determine whether an agency action is lawful under both New York law and the Administrative Procedure Act. . . . .

Without an evidentiary record, there is no reason to assume that New York courts applying this standard fail to provide license applicants with meaningful review. . . .

Second, the Court characterizes New York's proper cause standard as substantively "demanding." But, again, the Court has before it no evidentiary record to demonstrate how the standard has actually been applied. . . .

Finally, the Court compares New York's licensing regime to that of other States. It says that New York's law is a "may issue" licensing regime, which the Court describes as a law that provides licensing officers greater discretion to grant or deny licenses than a "shall issue" licensing regime. Because the Court counts 43 "shall issue" jurisdictions and only 7 "may issue" jurisdictions, it suggests that New York's law is an outlier. . . .

In drawing a line between "may issue" and "shall issue" licensing regimes, the Court ignores the degree of variation within and across these categories. Not all "may issue" regimes are necessarily alike, nor are all "shall issue" regimes. Conversely, not all "may issue" regimes are as different from the "shall issue" regimes as the Court assumes. For instance, the Court recognizes in a footnote that three States (Connecticut, Delaware, and Rhode Island) have statutes with discretionary criteria, like so-called "may issue" regimes do. But the Court nonetheless counts them among the 43 "shall issue" jurisdictions because, it says, these three States' laws operate in practice more like "shall issue" regimes.

As these three States demonstrate, the line between "may issue" and "shall issue" regimes is not as clear cut as the Court suggests, and that line depends at least in part on how statutory discretion is applied in practice. Here, because the

Court strikes down New York's law without affording the State an opportunity to develop an evidentiary record, we do not know how much discretion licensing officers in New York have in practice or how that discretion is exercised, let alone how the licensing regimes in the other six "may issue" jurisdictions operate. . . .

III.A. How does the Court justify striking down New York's law without first considering how it actually works on the ground and what purposes it serves? The Court does so by purporting to rely nearly exclusively on history. It requires "the government [to] affirmatively prove that its firearms regulation is part of the historical tradition that delimits the outer bounds of 'the right to keep and bear arms.'" Beyond this historical inquiry, the Court refuses to employ what it calls "means-end scrutiny." That is, it refuses to consider whether New York has a compelling interest in regulating the concealed carriage of handguns or whether New York's law is narrowly tailored to achieve that interest. Although I agree that history can often be a useful tool in determining the meaning and scope of constitutional provisions, I believe the Court's near-exclusive reliance on that single tool today goes much too far.

[Justice Breyer argued that the history-only approach of the majority opinion and its rejection of the tiered-scrutiny analysis adopted by the courts of appeals in the wake of *Heller* and *McDonald* was inconsistent with the Court's approach in both of those cases.]

. . . After concluding that the Second Amendment protects an individual right to possess a firearm for self-defense, the *Heller* Court added that that right is "not unlimited." It thus had to determine whether the District of Columbia's law, which banned handgun possession in the home, was a permissible regulation of the right. In answering that second question, it said: "Under *any of the standards of scrutiny that we have applied to enumerated constitutional rights*, banning from the home 'the most preferred firearm in the nation to "keep" and use for protection of one's home and family' would fail constitutional muster." That language makes clear that the *Heller* Court understood some form of means-end scrutiny to apply. It did not need to specify whether that scrutiny should be intermediate or strict because, in its view, the District's handgun ban was so "severe" that it would have failed either level of scrutiny. . . .

B. The Court's near-exclusive reliance on history is not only unnecessary, it is deeply impractical. It imposes a task on the lower courts that judges cannot easily accomplish. Judges understand well how to weigh a law's objectives (its "ends") against the methods used to achieve those objectives (its "means"). Judges are far less accustomed to resolving difficult historical questions. Courts are, after all, staffed by lawyers, not historians. Legal experts typically have little experience answering contested historical questions or applying those answers to resolve contemporary problems.

The Court's insistence that judges and lawyers rely nearly exclusively on history to interpret the Second Amendment thus raises a host of troubling questions. Consider, for example, the following. Do lower courts have the research resources necessary to conduct exhaustive historical analyses in every Second

Amendment case? What historical regulations and decisions qualify as representative analogues to modern laws? How will judges determine which historians have the better view of close historical questions? Will the meaning of the Second Amendment change if or when new historical evidence becomes available? And, most importantly, will the Court's approach permit judges to reach the outcomes they prefer and then cloak those outcomes in the language of history? . . .

[T]he Court's opinion today . . . gives the lower courts precious little guidance regarding how to resolve modern constitutional questions based almost solely on history. The Court declines to "provide an exhaustive survey of the features that render regulations relevantly similar under the Second Amendment." Other than noting that its history-only analysis is "neither a . . . straightjacket nor a . . . blank check," the Court offers little explanation of how stringently its test should be applied. Ironically, the only two "relevan[t]" metrics that the Court does identify are "how and why" a gun control regulation "burden[s the] right to armed self-defense." In other words, the Court believes that the most relevant metrics of comparison are a regulation's means (how) and ends (why)—even as it rejects the utility of means-end scrutiny. . . .

[E]ven under ideal conditions, historical evidence will often fail to provide clear answers to difficult questions. As an initial matter, many aspects of the history of firearms and their regulation are ambiguous, contradictory, or disputed. . . .

I fear that history will be an especially inadequate tool when it comes to modern cases presenting modern problems. Consider the Court's apparent preference for founding-era regulation. Our country confronted profoundly different problems during that time period than it does today. Society at the founding was "predominantly rural." In 1790, most of America's relatively small population of just four million people lived on farms or in small towns. Even New York City, the largest American city then, as it is now, had a population of just 33,000 people. Small founding-era towns are unlikely to have faced the same degrees and types of risks from gun violence as major metropolitan areas do today, so the types of regulations they adopted are unlikely to address modern needs. . . .

The Court's answer is that judges will simply have to employ "analogical reasoning." But, as I explained above, the Court does not provide clear guidance on how to apply such reasoning. Even seemingly straightforward historical restrictions on firearm use may prove surprisingly difficult to apply to modern circumstances. . . .

Although I hope—fervently—that future courts will be able to identify historical analogues supporting the validity of regulations that address new technologies, I fear that it will often prove difficult to identify analogous technological and social problems from Medieval England, the founding era, or the time period in which the Fourteenth Amendment was ratified. Laws addressing repeating crossbows, launcegays, dirks, dagges, skeines, stilladers, and other ancient weapons will be of little help to courts confronting modern problems. And as technological progress pushes our society ever further beyond the bounds of the Framers' imaginations, attempts at "analogical reasoning" will become increasingly tortured. In short, a standard that relies solely on history is unjustifiable and unworkable.

IV. Indeed, the Court's application of its history-only test in this case demonstrates the very pitfalls described above. The historical evidence reveals a 700-year Anglo-American tradition of regulating the public carriage of firearms in general, and concealed or concealable firearms in particular. The Court spends more than half of its opinion trying to discredit this tradition. But, in my view, the robust evidence of such a tradition cannot be so easily explained away. Laws regulating the public carriage of weapons existed in England as early as the 13th century and on this Continent since before the founding. Similar laws remained on the books through the ratifications of the Second and Fourteenth Amendments through to the present day. Many of those historical regulations imposed significantly stricter restrictions on public carriage than New York's licensing requirements do today. Thus, even applying the Court's history-only analysis, New York's law must be upheld because "historical precedent from before, during, and . . . after the founding evinces a comparable tradition of regulation."

[Justice Breyer reviewed the same historical evidence cited in the majority opinion, but drew the opposite lessons from that record.]

* * *

The historical examples of regulations similar to New York's licensing regime are legion. Closely analogous English laws were enacted beginning in the 13th century, and similar American regulations were passed during the colonial period, the founding era, the 19th century, and the 20th century. Not all of these laws were identical to New York's, but that is inevitable in an analysis that demands examination of seven centuries of history. At a minimum, the laws I have recounted *resembled* New York's law, similarly restricting the right to publicly carry weapons and serving roughly similar purposes. That is all that the Court's test, which allows and even encourages "analogical reasoning," purports to require.

In each instance, the Court finds a reason to discount the historical evidence's persuasive force. Some of the laws New York has identified are too old. But others are too recent. Still others did not last long enough. Some applied to too few people. Some were enacted for the wrong reasons. Some may have been based on a constitutional rationale that is now impossible to identify. Some arose in historically unique circumstances. And some are not sufficiently analogous to the licensing regime at issue here. But if the examples discussed above, taken together, do not show a tradition and history of regulation that supports the validity of New York's law, what could? Sadly, I do not know the answer to that question. What is worse, the Court appears to have no answer either. . . .

V. New York's Legislature considered the empirical evidence about gun violence and adopted a reasonable licensing law to regulate the concealed carriage of handguns in order to keep the people of New York safe. The Court today strikes down that law based only on the pleadings. It gives the State no opportunity to present evidence justifying its reasons for adopting the law or showing how the law actually operates in practice, and it does not so much as acknowledge these important considerations. Because I cannot agree with the Court's decision to strike New York's law down without allowing for discovery or the development of any evidentiary record, without considering the State's compelling interest in preventing gun violence and protecting the safety of its citizens, and without considering the potentially deadly consequences of its decision, I respectfully dissent.

NOTES AND PROBLEM

1. Standard of Review. *Heller* was notable for the Court's coy refusal to articulate a specific standard of review, other than to reject a deferential one; *Bruen* sees the majority reject tiered scrutiny and the courts of appeals' consensus that some form of intermediate scrutiny applied and adopt a "history and tradition" approach. In other words, it seems that the default is that restrictions on gun rights are presumptively violative of the Second Amendment unless the state can bear the burden of proving that its regulation is part of an historical tradition of gun regulation in the United States. Given that there *was* evidence of restrictions on public carrying discussed my the majority and the dissent, what quantum of historical evidence will satisfy this test?

2. Lower Courts. The lack of guidance from the Supreme Court post-*Heller* left the lower courts at sea when adjudicating Second Amendment cases. Do you think that *Bruen*'s newly articulated standard of review will make future cases easier for lower courts to decide, or more difficult? Justice Breyer's dissent highlighted at least four problems with the history-and-tradition approach. He noted that "the difficulties attendant to extensive historical analysis will be especially acute in the lower courts." Second, "the Court's opinion . . . compounds these problems, for it gives lower courts precious little guidance regarding how to resolve modern constitutional questions based almost solely on history." Third, "even under ideal conditions, historical evidence will often fail to provide clear answers to difficult questions." And finally, Breyer "fear[ed] that history will be an especially inadequate tool when it comes to modern cases presenting modern problems."

3. History, Tradition, and Technological Change. Given that firearms have evolved since the Founding and even since the end of the 19th century, what is a court to do when a law regulates an aspect of firearms unknown in earlier times, as Justice Breyer anticipated? Justice Thomas acknowledges that the application of the "history-and-tradition" standard will be difficult, and also acknowledges that there will be questions to which history and tradition will yield no definitive answers. Obviously, he wrote, "arms" includes those weapons undreamt of in the

18th century, and "[m]uch like we use history to determine which modern 'arms' are protected by the Second Amendment,"

> so too does history guide our consideration of modern regulations that were unimaginable at the founding. When confronting such present-day firearm regulations, this historical inquiry that courts must conduct will often involve reasoning by analogy—a commonplace task for any lawyer or judge. Like all analogical reasoning, determining whether a historical regulation is a proper analogue for a distinctly modern firearm regulation requires a determination of whether the two regulations are "relevantly similar." And because "[e]verything is similar in infinite ways to everything else," one needs "some metric enabling the analogizer to assess which similarities are important and which are not," For instance, a green truck and a green hat are relevantly similar if one's metric is "things that are green." They are not relevantly similar if the applicable metric is "things you can wear."
>
> While we do not now provide an exhaustive survey of the features that render regulations relevantly similar under the Second Amendment, we do think that *Heller* and *McDonald* point toward at least two metrics: how and why the regulations burden a law-abiding citizen's right to armed self-defense. As we stated in *Heller* and repeated in *McDonald*, "individual self-defense is 'the *central component*' of the Second Amendment right." Therefore, whether modern and historical regulations impose a comparable burden on the right of armed self-defense and whether that burden is comparably justified are " '*central*' " considerations when engaging in an analogical inquiry.
>
> To be clear, analogical reasoning under the Second Amendment is neither a regulatory straightjacket nor a regulatory blank check. On the one hand, courts should not "uphold every modern law that remotely resembles a historical analogue," because doing so "risk[s] endorsing outliers that our ancestors would never have accepted." On the other hand, analogical reasoning requires only that the government identify a well-established and representative historical *analogue*, not a historical *twin*. So even if a modern-day regulation is not a dead ringer for historical precursors, it still may be analogous enough to pass constitutional muster.

Justice Breyer expressed skepticism that would be a sufficient or workable approach.

> The Court's answer is that judges will simply have to employ "analogical reasoning." But, as I explained above, the Court does not provide clear guidance on how to apply such reasoning. Even seemingly straightforward historical restrictions on firearm use may prove surprisingly difficult to apply to modern circumstances. The Court affirms *Heller*'s recognition that States may forbid public carriage in "sensitive places." But what, in 21st-century New York City, may properly be considered a sensitive place? Presumably "legislative assemblies, polling places, and courthouses," which the Court tells us were among the "relatively few" places "where weapons were altogether prohibited" in the 18th and 19th centuries. On the other hand, the Court also tells us that "expanding the category of 'sensitive places' simply to all places of public congregation that are not isolated from law enforcement defines th[at] category . . . far too broadly." So where does that leave the many locations in a modern city with no obvious 18th- or 19th-century analogue?

What about subways, nightclubs, movie theaters, and sports stadiums? The Court does not say.

Although I hope—fervently—that future courts will be able to identify historical analogues supporting the validity of regulations that address new technologies, I fear that it will often prove difficult to identify analogous technological and social problems from Medieval England, the founding era, or the time period in which the Fourteenth Amendment was ratified. Laws addressing repeating crossbows, launcegays, dirks, dagges, skeines, stilladers, and other ancient weapons will be of little help to courts confronting modern problems. And as technological progress pushes our society ever further beyond the bounds of the Framers' imaginations, attempts at "analogical reasoning" will become increasingly tortured. In short, a standard that relies solely on history is unjustifiable and unworkable.

4. A Better Alternative? Could the difficulties Justice Breyer highlights be avoided had the Court embraced the kind of tiered scrutiny that is a common feature of its other individual rights doctrines? Despite his *Heller* dissent, which seemed to favor a more deferential interest balancing approach, his *Bruen* dissent seems almost to have welcomed the adoption of strict scrutiny in Second Amendment cases as opposed to the history-and-tradition test the majority adopted. "Courts," he wrote, "must be permitted to consider the State's interest in preventing gun violence, the effectiveness of the contested law in achieving that interest, the degree to which the law burdens the Second Amendment right, and, if appropriate, any less restrictive alternatives." If you were a district court judge or a judge on the court of appeals, and you were hearing a Second Amendment challenge to a state law banning high-capacity magazines, which approach would you rather apply?

5. Problem. Assume that New York would like to regulate its issuance of concealed carry permits to the greatest degree that the Second Amendment would allow. How far could it go? Could it require a psychological evaluation as a precondition for issuance? Proof of training? Passing a test on state laws regarding the use of force in self-defense?